twice-knit knitting

by lee gilchrist

Published in
association with
Parade magazine

GROSSET & DUNLAP

A NATIONAL GENERAL COMPANY

Publishers • New York

**Photo credits: Designs and fashions—Randy Ryoti,
Marquette, Michigan**

**Stitch illustrations—Fred Lillpopp,
Cheshire, Mass.**

CONTENTS

INTRODUCTION

TWICE-KNIT is a knitting method whereby each stitch is locked in place by virtue of the fact that each stitch is knitted through its neighbor stitch—thus, a stitch is worked through twice but moved only *once*.

Qualities of TWICE-KNIT are as follows:

I. Interlocked stitches

  a. Snag proof
  b. Run proof
  c. No unravelling when cut

Should a stitch become caught, the stitches on either side of the snag will not tighten and a quick "pop" of the knit will return the snagged stitch to its original shape and position.

The stitches can be removed from the needle without binding-off and will not drop down, causing a run. When cut like fabric, perfect loops result across the top and bottom of the knit and will not run up or down the knit. Of course, if the working end yarn is pulled the knit will unravel. The end yarn should always be secured before removing the knit from needles without utilizing the bind-off process.

When a thread is pulled horizontally after cutting the knit, a small knot will form on the edge and none of the stitches in the row will tighten. (When a thread is pulled horizontally in conventional knit, the item is divided into two pieces.)

These facts enable the knitter to shorten an item, cut buttonholes, or actually use the knit as yard goods without fear of runs or unravelling.

II. Fabric Appearance

The stitches are turned in such a manner that only one side of the loop is visible on the front of the knit and the other side of the loop is visible on the back of the knit. The result is a firmer knit with a look of fabric.

III. Gauge

On the three basic stitches—double back knit, double front knit, and double purl—the stitch gauge is determined by the width of the yarn rather than the size of the needle. The number of rows knitted per inch is determined by the size of the needle and generally remains the same for each needle size regardless of the size yarn used. The exception to the rule would be in using a yarn which is exceptionally elastic. The number of stitches per inch remain the same per type of yarn used regardless of the size needle used, i.e., knitted worsted—4 ply—gives 6 stitches per inch whether knit on size 11 or size 13 or size 15 needle.

IV. Shape retainability

TWICE-KNIT does not stretch lengthwise. Each stitch is elongated to its fullest while knitting. Thus, it is important to remember to knit the item the exact length that you desire the finished product to be. For example, a skirt is normally knit one inch shorter than desired to allow for the stretch which occurs when wearing. Not so with TWICE-KNIT. This feature also enables a knitter to use the largest of the jumbo needles and finer yarns without fear that it will grow as it is used.

There is less give to the knit when it is purposely pulled or stretched since it is a form of double knit and is a much closer knit. When it is stretched sideways from wearing, pull lengthwise on the knit and regain the original shape. Because Twice-Knit items don't stretch, you can knit and wear clothing without the extra cost and work of lining the item.

V. Denser Form of Knit.

Since the knit is a form of double knit, a much larger needle is required to give the same texture of conventional knitting. The smaller the needle the tighter the knit.

Finer type yarns such as for dresses and socks can be knit on larger needles without giving a too-loose appearance. This can be classified as a "quick-knit" for fine yarns.

The dense quality of the knit allows many items to be knit which are not feasible in conventional knit. Items considered of a heavy fabric nature, such as top coats, blankets, bedspreads, chair seats, upholstery fabric, etc., are in this category. Here I might add that only a single strand of yarn is necessary when knitting such weighty objects. TWICE-KNIT can also be knitted loose enough, by using larger needles, to make all of the standard and lighter weight items, such as sweater, socks, dresses, hats, scarves, etc.

VI. Color changes.

Each stitch is interlocked with its neighbor stitch as it is knit; therefore, it is not necessary to carry a color across the next stitch when changing colors. This is done automatically in the normal course of knitting TWICE-KNIT. You need only to pick up the next color and start knitting.

VII. Tieing-in Yarn.

It is not necessary to knot the ending yarn end and the beginning yarn end. Since the ending yarn end is already worked through the next stitch to be knitted, one need only to pick up the beginning yarn end and start working it. Then the yarn ends are worked into the reverse side of the work after completion of the item. This is possible because the knit will not run or unravel.

VIII. Design Possibilities.

The design possibilities are unlimited. The three basic stitches can be combined in numerous ways to create various fabric patterns. The look of TWICE-KNIT is totally different from conventional knit. It must be kept in mind that it has a look of fabric rather than knit; therefore, each stitch combination has a completely different appearance than conventional knit stitch combinations. ∎

TWICE-KNIT ABBREVIATIONS

B	Back
F	Front
DP	Double Purl
DFK	Double Front Knit
DBK	Double Back Knit
K	Knit
BK	Back Knit
P	Purl
RP	Reverse Purl
Sl	Slip
tog	together
inc	increase
dec	decrease
st (s)	stitch (es)
DP2tog	Double Purl two together
DFK2tog	Double Front Knit two together
DBK2tog	Double Back Knit two together
DK2tog	Double Knit two together
DK2togFB	Double Knit two together front and back
K2tog	Knit two together
K2togFB	Knit two together front and back
P2tog	Purl two together
K3togFBF	Knit three together front, back and front
K3togBFB	Knit three together back, front and back
Y.O.	Yarn over
Y. B.	Yarn back
Y.F.	Yarn front

DBK2tog (D1, SL1)—Double Back Knit two together, but instead of removing two stitches from the left needle, remove 1 stitch and slip one to the right needle.

DP2tog (D1, Sl1)—Double Purl two together, but instead of removing two from the left needle, remove the first one and slip the second one to the right needle.

5

TRICKS OF THE TRADE

As in any endeavor, there are certain "tricks" to knitting which not only make it easier and more of a pleasure but also improve the appearance. This is certainly true of TWICE-KNIT. Each of the items in this book can be accomplished in any number of ways; however, these are the things that make knitting easy for me and perhaps can do the same for you.

I. One of the most frequently asked questions is how to keep the end stitch from being too loose and looking quite ugly. One very simple way to cure this problem is to leave the first stitch worked onto the right needle on the point of the needle. Work the second stitch and then push the two of them together back off the point and onto the regular part of the needle.

Another way to keep the end stitch pretty and to also

6

form a non-giving edge (one that does not have to be crocheted around) is to knit through three stitches: drop the first one off the needle, slip the second one to the right needle, continue across the row in pattern to the last two stitches, knit through the two stitches, drop the first one off the needle and slip the second one to the right needle. Try it—it works!

II. Having to work the yarn ends into the back of the work once an item is completed is quite a nuisance. This can be avoided by carrying the beginning yarn end of the next strand across the back of the work as you work the last six or eight stitches of the ending yarn end. Then carry the ending yarn end across the back of the work as you work the first six or eight stitches of the new strand of yarn. If you find it difficult to carry yarn across behind the work, simply thread the new yarn end thru a darning needle and work it through the back of the work. Thread the ending yarn end thru the needle and work it thru the back of the work. Begin knitting with the new strand of yarn. REMEMBER! With TWICE-KNIT it is not necessary to tie the yarn ends together.

III. Quite often the bind-off process is either much too tight or much too loose. Also it is a problem just what to do with the last stitch to keep it from sticking out the edge like an afterthought. If this is one of your problems, go ahead and work the last row of the pattern without binding-off. Remove the needle from the work and reverse it. Now, slip the first three stitches onto the point of the right needle. Pass the first stitch slipped over the other two. Leaving the two stitches on the point of the right needle, slip one more stitch to the right needle and repeat the passing over process. Continue across the row until three stitches remain on the left needle. Pass the last two stitches over the first one and slip the one remaining stitch to the right needle. Pass the last two stitches on the right needle over the first one; break the yarn and pull it thru the remaining stitch on the right needle. Granted, this is more time consuming than the process of binding-off as you work the last row; however, if it is the only way you can get a bind-off that is as even and as pretty as the knit-on (or cast-on) edge, it is well worth the time and trouble.

IV. About the only mistake that is possible in TWICE-KNIT is to drop off both the stitches when knitting thru them instead of just one. If you do not catch this mistake as it happens, it will be quite obvious on the next row because the dropped stitch and the one next to it will not be interlocked. To correct this situation you remove the needles from the work and unravel the row being worked and the row with the mistake. Replace the stitches on the needle and continue. This is not as frightening as it sounds because the stitches in TWICE-KNIT will not run down and when you unravel back several rows, the row being picked up will have the same size stitch as when it was knitted. In conventional knit the stitches have a tendency to tighten once they have been worked and removed from the needle. Thus, these stitches quite often have to be picked up on a smaller needle. Not so with TWICE-KNIT. I feel that is another nice advantage, don't you?

V. This perhaps has nothing to do with the "tricks of the trade," but it is important to the beginning knitter to understand why the hands have a tendency to ache. Knitting is the same as any endeavor that you are undertaking for the first time. Perhaps I should not limit myself to the beginning knitter because even the most experienced knitter will be doing TWICE-KNIT for the first time. Therefore it is a new and strange experience and one which will cause a certain degree of tension. Tension causes one to hold the hands rather rigid and thus the muscles will start to ache after even a short time. Once you are familiar with the new process and it comes easy and natural to you, you will relax and the aching will be over and done.

VI. I was always taught, and perhaps you were also, that machine stitching hand-knits together was taboo. TWICE-KNIT has such shape retainability and sewing machines have improved over the years to such a fantastic degree that I advocate machine stitching together the individual pieces rather than have an item poorly put together by hand. Some people do not have that certain "knack" that it takes to beautifully finish a garment by hand. TWICE-KNIT has the texture of fabric and can be treated as such without taking away from the beauty of the hand-knit appearance. Items such as bedspreads which need a certain amount of durability are actually much better when machine stitched. Also, since TWICE-KNIT does not stretch lengthwise, sweaters, dresses, coats and the like may be machine sewed together without having to worry about the rest of the item stretching and the seam remaining rigid.

VII. One question asked by everyone the minute they hear the name "TWICE-KNIT" is whether it takes twice the yarn. Not only does it not take twice the yarn, but in many instances it does not take as much yarn. The closeness of the stitch dictates more stitches per inch, but the large size of the needle dictates fewer rows per inch. To obtain the same weight item knit on a #8 needle with 4-ply knitted worsted yarn in conventional knit, you would use a #13 or perhaps a #15 needle in TWICE-KNIT. This I believe is a reasonable comparison of stitches worked per square inch. Conventional Knit—Gauge— 9 sts = 2″, 6 rows = 1″. Total stitches worked over a 2″ square equals 108 sts. TWICE-KNIT—Gauge—6 sts =1″, 7 rows = 2″. Total stitches worked over a 2″ square equals 84 sts. With a #15 needle there would be a total of 72 sts worked. One might surmise that once a knitter became as familiar with TWICE-KNIT as she was with conventional knit that it would be a faster form of knit since fewer stitches had to be moved to complete the process.

Perhaps I have not touched on the one knitting problem

that might be causing you trouble, but if only one of the suggestions given makes knitting more of a pleasure for you, then the time it took to jot them down was well spent.

DOUBLE KNIT-ON
PROCEDURE

Double Knit-On is the procedure used in placing the original stitches on the needle; that is, a method of beginning the knitting. The procedure in conventional knitting would be known as casting on.

Fig. 1 To begin the process, a slip-knot is placed on the left needle.

Fig. 2 The right needle is inserted from left to right thru the slip knot and the yarn wrapped around the right needle point.

Fig. 3 The new stitch is pulled through the slip-knot.

Fig. 1   **Fig. 2**   **Fig. 3**

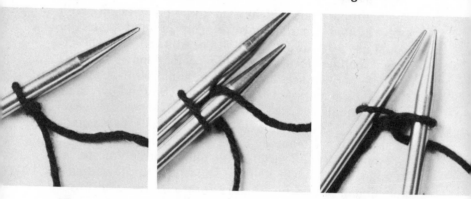

Fig. 4 The new stitch is transferred from the right needle to the left needle and there are now two stitches on the

left needle.

Fig. 5 The right needle is inserted from left to right thru the two stitches on the left needle and the yarn wrapped around the right needle point.

Fig. 4   Fig. 5

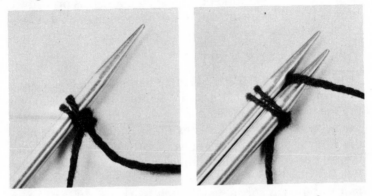

Fig. 6 The newly formed stitch is pulled thru the two stitches on the left needle. As with the first stitch, this stitch is also transferred from the right needle to the left needle. There are now three stitches on the left needle.

Fig. 7 This stitch and all subsequent stitches to be knitted-on will be worked by inserting the right needle point thru the first two stitches on the left needle from left to right,

Fig. 6   Fig. 7

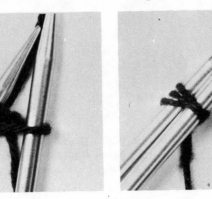

wrap the yarn around the right needle point and pull it thru the two stitches. As in the previous steps, the stitch is then transferred from the right needle to the left.

By placing the original stitches on the needle in this manner, your tension gauge will be the same as the subsequent rows of knitted or purled stitches. This procedure allows the first row of knit to be loose enough on the needle to be worked easily.

DOUBLE BACK KNIT

Double Back Knit (DBK). Insert needle in back side thru first and second stitches and knit thru the two. Remove the first stitch only of the two worked stitches. This leaves the second of the two stitches remaining on the left needle and already worked once. Knit thru that stitch and the one next to it thru the back and remove it from the left needle. This stitch just removed has been worked twice and each subsequent stitch worked in this manner will have been worked twice before being removed from the left needle.

Fig. 1   **Fig. 2**   **Fig. 3**

Fig. 1 Insert right needle point from right to left thru the back of the first two stitches on the left needle. Loop yarn around the right needle point and pull through the two stitches.

Fig. 2 Position of the yarn after it has been pulled thru the two stitches and before one has been removed from the left needle.

Fig. 3 Position of the yarn after the first stitch has been removed—this completes double back knit stitch.

NOTE: The last single stitch remaining on the left needle when doing a row of double back knit is worked as a single back knit stitch or if a tight edge is desired, the stitch may be reversed and slipped to the right needle.

DOUBLE FRONT KNIT

Double Front Knit (DFK). Knit thru the front of two stitches, inserting the needle from left to right, removing only one of the two worked stitches from the left needle each time.

Fig. 1 Insert point of right needle from left to right thru the front of the first two stitches on left needle. Wrap yarn around right needle point as shown and pull thru the two stitches.

Fig. 2 Position of yarn after stitch has been pulled thru the two stitches but none of the stitches have been removed from left needle.

Fig. 3 Position after first stitch on left needle has been removed.

Fig. 1　　　　**Fig. 2**　　　　**Fig. 3**

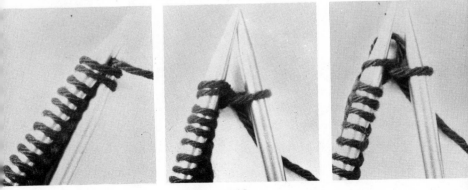

NOTE: The working yarn is thru the first stitch now on the left needle and will always be attached to the first stitch of the left needle when working a double front knit stitch.

Continue repeating the steps outlined in Figures 1 thru 3 to double front knit across a row. There will remain one stitch on the left needle at the end of a row. This stitch is to be worked as a regular front knit stitch.

DOUBLE PURL

Double Purl (DP). Insert needle from right to left thru the front of the first two stitches on the left needle, wrap yarn around the point of the right needle and pull thru the two stitches. Remove the first stitch of the two worked stitches from the left needle.

Fig. 1 Insert right needle point thru the first two stitches on left needle from right to left as shown. Wrap yarn around right needle point and pull thru the two stitches.

Fig. 1   **Fig. 2**   **Fig. 3**

Fig. 2 Position of yarn and stitches after the new stitch has been worked but the first stitch on the left needle has not yet been removed.

Fig. 3 Position of yarn and stitches after the removal of the first of the two worked stitches on the left needle has been removed.

NOTE: The position of the working yarn is thru the first stitch of the left needle and will always be thus positioned when working a double purl stitch.

Continue to repeat the above procedure when working a complete row of double purl. There will remain one stitch on the left needle when a row has been worked. This stitch is worked as a regular purl stitch.

KNIT TWO TOGETHER FRONT AND BACK

Knit Two Together Front and Back (K2togFB). Knit two stitches together in the front of the needle and without removing either of the two stitches from the left needle, knit the same two stitches together through the back of the stitches. Now remove the two worked stitches from the left needle.

Fig. 1 Insert right needle thru the front of the first two stitches from left to right as shown. Loop yarn around right needle point and pull thru the two stitches.

Fig. 2 Position of yarn after it has been pulled thru the two stitches shown in Fig. 1. Do not remove stitches from left needle.

Fig. 3 With yarn brought to the back of your work, insert right needle point from right to left thru the back of the

| Fig. 1 | Fig. 2 | Fig. 3 |

same two stitches shown in Fig. 1. Loop yarn around right needle point and pull thru the two stitches.

Fig. 4 Position of the yarn after it has been pulled thru the stitches shown in Fig. 3. The two stitches which were worked thru have not yet been removed from the left needle.

Fig. 5 The two stitches worked thru have now been removed from the left needle. Two new stitches are now added to the right needle.

Fig. 4   **Fig. 5**

The above steps complete the necessary procedure for the K2togFB stitch. This stitch is not one of the basic stitches of Twice-Knit; therefore, it is not included in the non-run, non-snag category. It does add a decorative stitch which is complimentary to the stitches in Twice-Knit.

BINDING-OFF IN TWICE-KNIT

The binding-off process in Twice-Knit is much the same as in conventional knit with the exception that you are working double knit stitches or double purl stitches and therefore a much closer form of knit. Thus the bind-off must be in accordance and be of a tighter form. For this

16

reason, instead of passing one stitch over one stitch to bind-off, the procedure will be to pass one stitch over two stitches.

Fig. 1 Work three stitches in pattern. As shown, there are three stitches now on the right needle.

Fig. 2 Insert the left needle point from left to right thru the front of the third stitch as shown, and pass this stitch over the other two stitches and off the right needle.

Fig. 3 Position of the stitches after the one stitch has been passed over the other two and removed from the needle.

Fig. 1   **Fig. 2**   **Fig. 3**

From this point on, each time you will work one more stitch in pattern, keeping a total of three stitches on the right needle. Each time there are three stitches on the right needle, repeat the process illustrated in Fig. 2. Continue in this manner until all stitches have been removed from the left needle or until the desired number of stitches have been bound-off. There will remain two stitches on the right needle at the end of the bind-off process. Pass the last stitch over the first stitch, break the yarn, and pull the yarn thru the last remaining stitch on the right needle.

NOTE: If you should be one of those individuals who naturally bind-off too tightly, then, by all means, use the conventional method of passing one stitch over one stitch.

SILHOUETTE STITCH

SILHOUETTE STITCH is made by alternating one row of Double Front Knit (DFK) and one row of Double Purl (DP). The right side will be the side facing you when working a row of Double Front Knit. The reverse side or wrong side will be facing you when working a row of Double Purl. When the Double Purl side is used for the right side, it will be referred to as "REVERSED SIL-HOUETTE STITCH."

Fig. 1. Silhouette Stitch
Fig. 2. Reversed Silhouette Stitch.

Fig. 1   **Fig. 2**

HERRINGBONE STITCH

HERRINGBONE STITCH is made by alternating one row of Double Back Knit (DBK) and one row of Double Purl (DP). The right side of the work is facing you when working a row of Double Back Knit. The reverse or wrong side of the work will be facing you when working a row of Double Purl. When the Double Purl side is used for the

18

right side, it will be referred to as "REVERSED HERR-
INGBONE STITCH."
Fig. 1. Herringbone Stitch
Fig. 2. Reversed Herringbone Stitch.

Fig. 1   **Fig. 2**

BRAID STITCH

BRAID STITCH can be accomplished in any one of three
methods.
Method 1. Double Back Knit (DBK) across to last st., BK 1.
Method 2. Double Front Knit (DFK) across to last st., K 1.
Method 3. Double Purl (DP) across to last st., P 1.
Any of the above Methods repeated continually will result

Fig. 1

in the Braid Stitch. This stitch is reversible—in other words, both sides are the same and either one may be considered the right side.

Fig. 1. Braid Stitch (Method 1).

GRAPHIC STITCH

GRAPHIC STITCH is a combination of the Herringbone and Silhouette stitches.

Row 1. Double Front Knit (DFK) across to last st., K 1.
Row 2. Double Purl (DP) across to last st., P 1.
Row 3. Double Back Knit (DBK) across to last st., BK 1.
Row 4. Double Purl (DP) across to last st., P 1.

The above 4 rows constitute the Graphic Stitch.

Fig. 1. Graphic Stitch
Fig. 2. Reversed Graphic Stitch

Fig. 1   **Fig. 2**

PROCEDURES

DECREASING IN TWICE-KNIT The procedure for decreasing is the same for all of the three basic stitches. The abbreviations differ to indicate the particular stitch being used. To decrease work thru three stitches and drop off two stitches.

DBK2tog—Double Back Knit two together—Knit thru the back of three stitches and drop off two.

DFK2tog—Double Front Knit two together—Knit thru the front of three stitches and drop off two.

DP2tog—Double Purl two together—Purl thru three stitches and drop off two.

INCREASING IN TWICE-KNIT The procedure for increasing in each of the stitches varies. It also varies whether you are increasing at the beginning of the row or in the center.

DBK—Double Back Knit—Increasing at the beginning of the row.

Method 1. Knit thru the back of the first stitch and without removing it from the needle, work a regular double back knit stitch.

Method 2. Knit thru the back of two stitches and instead of removing one, slip it to the right needle.

INCREASING IN THE MIDDLE OF THE ROW Knit thru the back of three stitches and without removing any from the left needle, work a regular double back knit stitch.

DFK—Double Front Knit—Increasing at the beginning of the row. Knit thru the front of the first stitch and without removing it from the needle, work a regular double front knit stitch.

INCREASING IN THE MIDDLE OF THE ROW Same as increasing at the beginning of the row.

DP—Double Purl—Increasing at the beginning of the row.

Method 1. Purl thru the front of the first stitch and without removing it from the needle, work a regular double purl stitch.

Method 2. Purl thru the front of two stitches and instead of removing one, slip it to the right needle.

INCREASING IN THE MIDDLE OF THE ROW - Purl thru the front of three stitches and without removing any from the left needle, work a regular double purl stitch.

There are many ways of increasing and decreasing that are similiar to the above methods. These to me were the easiest. Actually, a very nice increase is to simply work a double stitch thru the same two stitches twice before removing one as in a regular double stitch. This perhaps is a more obvious form of increase, but is quite easy to negotiate.

BABY BLANKET
Approx. size 30″ x 34″

MATERIAL: 4 - 4 oz. Skeins Coats & Clark's Red Heart "Sayelle"
1 Circular Needle Size #11

GAUGE: 11 sts = 2″   9 rows = 2″

Double Knit-On 164 sts.

Row 1 . . . DFK across to last st., K 1.

Row 2 . . . DP across to last st., P 1.

Rows 3 & 5 . . . Repeat Row 1.

Rows 4 & 6 . . . Repeat Row 2.

Row 7 . . . DFK 8, place marker, K2togFB across the next 70 sts, place marker, DFK 8, place marker, K2togFB across the next 70 sts, place marker DFK 7, K 1.

Row 8 . . . DP across to last st., P 1.

Rows 9 thru 38 . . . Repeat Rows 7 & 8 alternately.

The above 38 rows complete one design section.

Repeat these 38 rows 3 more times. There are now a total of 152 rows worked.

Rows 153, 155 & 157 . . . Repeat Row 1.

Rows 154 & 156 . . . Repeat Row 2.

Row 158 . . . Bind-off while repeating Row 2.

FINISHING: Fringe around entire blanket using 3 - 5″ strands of yarn per single fringe. Fringe in every other stitch. Blocking not necessary.

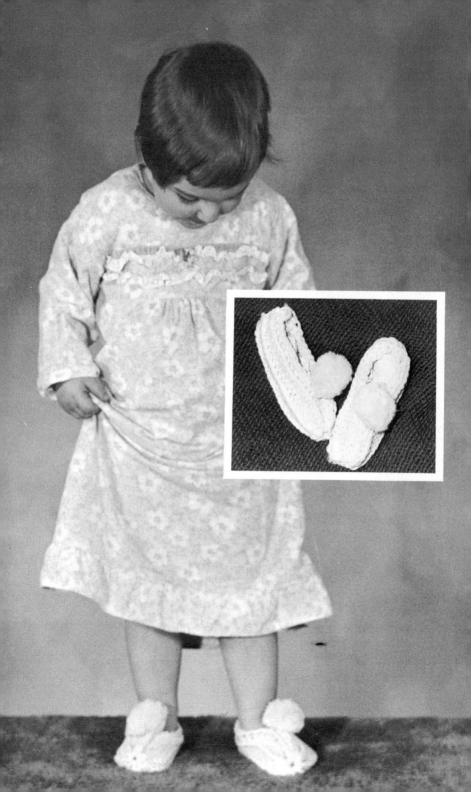

TODDLER'S SLIPPER

MATERIAL: Approx. ½ oz. Phentex Yarn
                     1 pr. #17 Needles (½″)
GAUGE: 4 sts = 1″   2 rows = 1′
Slipper sized for 1-3 years. Knit 2.
Double Knit-On 24 sts.
Braid Pattern.
Row 1 . . . DBK across to last st., BK 1.
Repeat Row 1 until a total of 13 rows have been worked.
Row 14 . . . Bind-off as you repeat Row 1.
FINISHING: Fold in half, placing bind-off edge and knit-on edge together. Seam the end to be the heel of the slipper. Run a gathering thread thru the end to be the toe of the slipper and pull together tightly. Secure. From the toe, sew the bind-off edge and the knit-on edge together for approximately 2″. Make a 1″ pom-pom and attach to the top of the slipper. Work in yarn ends. No blocking necessary.

DOLL'S SCARF & HAT

MATERIAL: Approx. ½ oz. 4 - Ply Knitting Worsted
                  Colors A & B.
                  1 pr. #13 Needles
GAUGE: 6 sts = 1″   7 rows = 2″
SCARF—Braid Pattern
Double Knit-On 20 sts using Color A.
Row 1 . . . DBK across to last st., BK 1.
Repeat Row 1 until a total of 50 rows have been worked or until desired length.
Bind-off repeating Row 1.
FINISHING: Single crochet around the scarf using Color B. Block to size.
HAT—Braid Pattern
Double Knit-On 36 sts using Color B.
Row 1 . . . DBK across to last st., BK 1.
Repeat Row 1 until a total of 40 rows have been worked or until hat measures the same as the doll's head mea-

surement.

Bind-off repeating Row 1.

FINISHING: Block. Sew the bind-off and the knit-on edges together. Run a gathering thread around one of the open ends—draw tightly and secure. Work in yarn ends.

BOY'S HAT & SCARF SET

MATERIAL: 2 Skeins Phentex Yarn
1 pr. #17 Needles (½″)

GAUGE: 4 sts = 1″   5 rows = 2″

HAT:

Double Knit-On 40 sts.

Row 1 . . . DBK across to last st., BK 1.

Row 2 . . . DBK 18, DP across to last st., P 1.

Rows 3-44 . . . Repeat Rows 1 & 2.

Row 45 . . . Repeat Row 1.

Row 46 . . . Bind-off while repeating Row 2.

FINISHING: Sew Knit-On and Bind-off edges together. Run a thread thru the end stitches of the plain end. Draw

tightly into a circle and secure on the reverse side. Turn
back 2″ ribbed cuff. No blocking necessary.

SCARF:

Double Knit-On 168 sts. (Scarf is worked lengthwise)

Row 1 . . . DBK across to last st., BK 1.

Row 2 . . . DBK 18, DP to within last 18 sts., DBK 17, BK 1.

Rows 3-12 . . . Repeat Rows 1 & 2.

Row 13 . . . Repeat Row 1.

Row 14 . . . Bind-off by passing 1 st over 1 st while repeating Row 2.

FINISHING: Work in yarn ends. Block.

LITTLE GIRL'S PEEK-A-BOO HAT

This hat matches the Child's Maxi-Scarf in design.

MATERIAL: 2 Skeins Phentex

                 1 pr. #17 Needles (½″)

GAUGE: 7 sts = 2″   2 rows = 1″

This hat is quite thick and can be made with 1 Skein of Phentex and a single strand of yarn, if desired.

With a double strand of yarn, Double Knit-On 72 sts.

Row 1 . . . DBK across to last st., BK 1.

Row 2 . . . DBK 18 *Y.O., DBK2tog*, repeat from * to * to last 4 sts., TURN.

Row 3 . . . Y.B., Sl 1, DBK across to last st., BK 1.

Row 4 . . . DBK 18, *Y.O., DBK2tog*, repeat from * to * to last 8 sts., TURN.

Row 5 . . . Y.B., Sl 1, DBK across to last st., BK 1.

Row 6 . . . DBK 18, *Y.O., DBK2tog*, repeat from * to * to last 12 sts., TURN.

Row 7 . . . Y.B., Sl 1, DBK across to last st., BK 1.

Row 8 . . . DBK 18, *Y.O., DBK2tog*, repeat from * to * to last 16 sts., TURN.

Row 9 . . . Y.B., Sl 1, DBK across to last st., BK 1.

Row 10 . . DBK 18, *Y.O., DBK2 tog*, repeat from * to * to last 20 sts., TURN.

Row 11 . . Y.B., Sl 1, DBK across to last st., BK 1.

Row 12 . . DBK 18, *Y.O. DBK2tog*, repeat from * to * to last 24 sts., TURN.

Row 13 . . Y.B., Sl 1, DBK across to last st., BK 1.

Row 14 . . DBK 18, *Y.O., DBK2tog*, repeat from * to * to last 28 sts., TURN.

Row 15 . . Y.B., Sl 1, DBK across to last st., BK 1.

Row 16 . . DBK 18, *Y.O. DBK2tog*, repeat from * to * to last 32 sts., TURN.

Row 17 . . Y.B., Sl 1, DBK across to last st., BK 1.

Row 18 . . DBK 18, *Y.O., DBK2tog*, repeat from * to * to last 36 sts., TURN.

Row 19 . . Y.B., Sl 1, DBK across to last st., BK 1.

Row 20 . . DBK 18, *Y.O., DBK2tog*, repeat from * to * to last 36 sts., TURN.

Row 21 . . Y.B., Sl 1, DBK across to last st., BK 1.

Row 22 . . DBK 18, *Y.O., DBK2tog*, repeat from * to * to last 32 sts, TURN.

Row 23 . . Y.B., Sl 1, DBK across to last st., BK 1.

Row 24 . . DBK 18, *Y.O., DBK2tog*, repeat from * to * to last 28 sts., TURN.

Row 25 . . Y.B., Sl 1, DBK across to last st., BK 1.

Row 26 . . DBK 18, *Y.O., DBK2tog*, repeat from * to * to last 24 sts., TURN.

Row 27 . . Y.B., Sl 1, DBK across to last st., BK 1.

Row 28 . . DBK 18, *Y.O., DBK2tog*, repeat from * to * to last 20 sts., TURN.

Row 29 . . Y.B., Sl 1, DBK across to last st., BK 1.

Row 30 . . DBK 18, *Y.O., DBK2tog*, repeat from * to * to last 16 sts., TURN.

Row 31 . . Y.B., Sl 1, DBK across to last st., BK 1.

Row 32 . . DBK 18, *Y.O., DBK2tog*, repeat from * to * to last 12 sts., TURN.

Row 33 . . Y.B., Sl 1, DBK across to last st., TURN.

Row 34 . . DBK 18, *Y.O., DBK2tog*, repeat from * to * to last 8 sts., TURN.

Row 35 . . Y.B., Sl 1, DBK across to last st., BK 1.

Row 36 . . DBK 18, *Y.O., DBK2tog*, repeat from * to * to last 4 sts., TURN.

Row 37 . . Y.B., Sl 1, DBK across to last st., BK 1.

Row 38 . . Bind-off . . DBK 18, reverse the next st so that yarn is in front, DP to end of row.

FINISHING: Block. Sew the knit-on and bind-off edges of the 18 rib stitches and the first 18 stitches of the design pattern together. Attach a 5″ tassel made from 24 - 11″ pieces of yarn to the tip end of the hat. Work in yarn ends.

CHILD'S MAXI SCARF

MATERIAL: 1—3.2 oz. Skein Phentex
               1—pr. #17 Needles (½″)
GAUGE: 3 sts = 1″   5 rows = 2″
Double Knit-On 240 sts.
PATTERN:
Row 1 . . .   DBK across to last st., BK 1.

Row 2 . . . DBK 18, *Y.O., DBK2tog*, repeat from * to * to last 18 sts., DBK 17, BK 1.

Repeat Rows 1 & 2 until a total of 12 rows have been worked.

Row 13 . . . Bind-off in DBK.

FINISHING: Block—pin scarf to correct size—5˝ x 84˝— wet thoroughly and let dry completely. If steam is used, never let the iron touch the knit. Heat will scorch and harden the yarn.

Draw a thread thru each end gathering the ribs and draw them as tightly as possible. Attach 5˝ tassels made from 24—11˝ pieces of yarn.

TURTLE NECK EAR WARMER

MATERIAL: 1—4 oz. Skein Coats & Clark's Red Heart Knitted Worsted—4-Ply
1 Circular Needle Size # 13 (used as a straight needle)

GAUGE: 6 sts = 1˝   7 rows = 2˝

Double Knit-On 30 sts.

Rows 1—24 . . . DBK across to last st., BK 1.

Double Knit-On an additional 96 sts. Carefully cut off the beginning knit-on edge and place the 30 sts on the other end of the needle so that they may be knitted onto the 112 sts already on the needle.

DBK across the 30 sts . . . there are now 156 sts on the needle.

Row 25 . . . DBK across to last st., BK 1.

Row 26 . . . DBK 30, place marker, DP to within last 30 sts., place marker, DBK 29, BK 1.

Row 27—39 . . . Repeat Rows 25 & 26 alternately, slipping the markers each time instead of placing markers.

Row 40 . . . DBK 30, Bind-off 96 sts in DBK, DBK 29, BK 1.

Working across the last 30 sts only . . .

Row 41 . . . DBK across to last st., BK 1.

Row 42—48 . . . Repeat Row 41.

Place the two sets of 30 sts in every other sequence and with right sides together, bind-off together on the reverse side using the following bind-off pattern: DBK thru 4 sts removing 2 each time. When three sts are on the right needle, pass 1 st over 2 sts until all stitches are removed. Pull yarn end thru last 2 sts on right needle and work yarn end into reverse side of the work. No blocking necessary.

HEADBAND

MATERIAL: Approx. ½ oz. Coats & Clark's Red Heart
Knitting Worsted 4-Ply
1 pr. #15 Needles

GUAGE: 6 sts = 1″   3 rows = 1″

Double Knit-On 12 sts.
Silhouette Pattern.

Row 1 . . . DFK across to last st., K 1.
Row 2 . . . DP across to last st., P 1.
Repeat Rows 1 & 2 until length measures 20″.
Bind-off in pattern.
FINISHING: Block to size. Sew bind-off edge and knit-on edges together. Work yarn ends into back of work.

SKI CAP

MATERIAL: Coats & Clark's Red Heart Knitting Worsted 4-Ply
1—1 oz. Skein each of Black, Scarlet, Canary Yellow and Emerald
1 pr. #11 Needles

GAUGE: 6 sts = 1″   4 rows = 1″

Double Knit-On 72 sts in Black.
Row 1 . . . Black . . . DBK across to last st., BK 1.
Row 2 . . . Black . . . DBK across to last st., BK 1.
Row 3 . . . Black . . . DBK 18 . . . change to . . . Scarlet . . . DBK across to last st., BK 1.
Row 4 . . . Scarlet . . . DP 54 . . . change to . . . Black . . . DBK across to last st., BK 1.
Rows 5—10 . . . Repeat Rows 3 & 4 Alternately.
Rows 11 & 12 . . . Repeat Row 1.
Row 13 . . . Black . . . DBK 18 . . . change to . . . Yellow . . . DBK across to last st., BK 1.
Row 14 . . . Yellow . . . DP 54 . . . change to . . . Black . . . DBK across to last st., BK 1.
Rows 15—20 . . . Repeat Rows 13 & 14 alternately.
Rows 21 & 22 . . . Repeat Row 1.
Row 23 . . . Black . . . DBK 18 . . . change to . . . Emerald . . . DBK across to last st., BK 1.
Row 24 . . . Emerald . . . DP 54 . . . change to . . . Black . . . DBK across to last st., BK 1.
Rows 25—30 . . . Repeat Rows 23 & 24 alternately.
Rows 31—90 . . . Repeat Rows 1—30 twice.
Row 91 . . . Bind-off in Black in DBK.
FINISHING: See finishing directions for Rainbow Cap on pages 40 and 41.

MATCHING SCARF FOR SKI CAP
Approx. size 8˝ x 60˝

MATERIAL: Coats & Clark's Red Heart Knitting
Worsted—4-Ply
1 —#11 Circular Needle

GAUGE: 6 sts = 1˝ 4 rows = 1˝

Double Knit-On 360 sts. (The scarf is worked lengthwise.)
Row 1 . . . Black . . . DBK across to last st., BK 1.
Row 2 . . . Black . . . Repeat Row 1.
Row 3 . . . Black . . . DBK 36, change to Red, DBK across to last 36 sts., change to Black, DBK 35, BK 1.
Row 4 . . . Black . . . DBK 36, change to Red, DP across to last 36 sts., change to Black, DBK 35, BK 1.
Rows 5, 7, 9 . . . Repeat Row 3.
Rows 6, 8, 10 . . . Repeat Row 4.
Rows 11 & 12 . . . Repeat Row 1.
Row 13 . . . Black . . . DBK 36, change to Yellow, DBK across to last 36 sts., change to Black, DBK 35, BK 1.
Row 14 . . . Black . . . DBK 36, change to Yellow, DP across to last 36 sts., change to Black, DBK 35, BK 1.
Rows 15, 17, 19 . . . Repeat Row 13.
Rows 16, 18, 20 . . . Repeat Row 14.
Rows 21 & 22 . . . Repeat Row 1.
Row 23 . . . Black . . . DBK 36, change to Green, DBK across to last 36 sts., change to Black, DBK 35, BK 1.
Row 24 . . . Black . . . DBK 36, change to Green, DP across to last 36 sts., change to Black, DBK 35, BK 1.
Rows 25, 27, 29 . . . Repeat Row 23.
Rows 26, 28, 30 . . . Repeat Row 24.
Row 31 . . . Repeat Row 1.
Row 32 . . . Bind-off while repeating Row 1.

FINISHING: Block to size. Work yarn ends into back of work.

RAINBOW CAP

MATERIAL: Coats & Clark's Red Heart Knitting
Worsted
1—1 oz. Skein each—Black, Scarlet, Lilac,
Skipper Blue, Emerald, Mid-Orange, Canary Yellow
1—pr. #11 Needles

GAUGE: 6 sts = 1″   4 rows = 1″
Double Knit-On 72 sts in Black.
Row 1 . . . Black . . . DBK across to last st., BK 1.
Row 2 . . . Black . . . DBK across to last st., BK 1.
Row 3 . . . Black . . . DBK 18 then change to . . . Red . . .
DBK across to last st., BK 1.
Row 4 . . . Red . . . DP 54 then change to : . . Black . . . DP
across to last st., P 1.
Row 5 . . . Black . . . DBK 18 then change to . . . Red . . . .
DBK across to last st., BK 1.
Row 6 . . . Red . . . DP 54 then change to . . . Black . . . DP
across to last st., P 1.
Row 7 . . . Black . . . DBK across to last st., BK 1.
Row 8 . . . Black . . . DBK across to last st., BK 1.
Row 9 . . . Black . . . DBK 18 then change to . . . Lilac . . :
DBK across to last st., BK 1.
Row 10 . . . Lilac . . . DP 54 then change to . . . Black . . .
DP across to last st., P 1.
Row 11 . . . Black . . . DBK 18 then change to . . . Lilac . . .
DBK across to last st., BK 1.
Row 12 . . . Lilac . . . DP 54 then change to . . . Black . . .
DP across to last st., P 1.
Row 13 . . . Black . . . DBK across to last st., BK 1.
Row 14 . . . Black . . . DBK across to last st., BK 1.
Row 15 . . . Black . . . DBK 18 then change to . . . Blue . . .
DBK across to last st., BK 1
Row 16 . . . Blue . . . DP 54 then change to . . . Black . . . DP
across to last st., P 1.
Row 17 . . . Black . . . DBK 18 then change to . . . Blue . . .
DBK across to last st., BK 1.

39

Row 18 . . . Blue . . . DP 54 then change to . . . Black . . . DP
across to last st., P 1.

Row 19 . . . Black . . . DBK across to last st., BK 1.

Row 20 . . . Black . . . DBK across to last st., BK 1.

Row 21 . . . Black . . . DBK 18 then change to . . . Emerald
. . . DBK across to last st., BK 1.

Row 22 . . . Emerald . . . DP 54 then change to . . . Black
. . . DP across to last st., P 1

Row 23 . . . Black . . . DBK 18, then change to . . . Emerald
. . . DBK across to last st., BK 1.

Row 24 . . . Emerald . . . DP 54 then change to . . . Black
. . . DP across to last st., P 1.

Row 25 . . . Black . . . DBK across to last st., BK 1.

Row 26 . . . Black . . . DBK across to last st., BK 1.

Row 27 . . . Black . . . DBK 18 then change to . . . Orange
. . . DBK across to last st., BK 1.

Row 28 . . . Orange . . . DP 54 then change to . . . Black . . .
DP across to last st., P 1.

Row 29 . . . Black . . . DBK 18, then change to . . . Orange
. . . DBK across to last st., BK 1.

Row 30 . . . Orange . . . DP 54 then change to . . . Black . . .
DP across to last st., P 1.

Row 31 . . . Black . . . DBK across to last st., BK 1.

Row 32 . . . Black . . . DBK across to last st., BK 1.

Row 33 . . . Black . . . DBK 18 then change to . . . Yellow
. . . DBK across to last st., BK 1.

Row 34 . . . Yellow . . . DP 54 then change to . . . Black . . .
DP across to last st., P 1.

Row 35 . . . Black . . . DBK 18 then change to . . . Yellow
. . . DBK across to last st., BK 1.

Row 36 . . . Yellow . . . DP 54 then change to . . . Black . . .
DP across to last st., P 1.

Repeat the above 36 rows twice more. Bind-off on Row 36
of the last repeat. There should be a total of 108 rows.

FINISHING: Sew the bind-off and the knit-on edges together with black yarn. Gather the striped edge together
tightly. Make a large pom-pom out of black and fasten it
over the gathered circle. Secure firmly. Work in all yarn

40

ends on the reverse side of work. The black ribbed edge can be turned back 2″-2½″ for a cuff effect or leave straight for a pull-on effect. No blocking necessary.

RAINBOW SCARF
Approx. size 8″ x 60″

MATERIAL: Coats & Clark's Red Heart Knitting Worsted
1—1 oz. Skein Each—Black, Scarlet, Lilac, Skipper Blue, Emerald, Mid-Orange, Canary Yellow
1 pr. #11 Needles
Crochet Hook Size F

GAUGE: 6 sts = 1″   4 rows = 1″
Double Knit-On 48 sts. in Black.

PATTERN: Combination of Braid and Herringbone.

Row 1 . . . Black . . . DBK across to last st., BK 1.
Row 2 . . . Black . . . DBK across to last st., BK 1.
Row 3 . . . Scarlet . . . DBK across to last st., BK 1.
Row 4 . . . Scarlet . . . DP across to last st., P 1.
Row 5 . . . Scarlet . . . DBK across to last st., BK 1.
Row 6 . . . Scarlet . . . DP across to last st., P 1.
Row 7 . . . Black . . . DBK across to last st., BK 1.
Row 8 . . . Black . . . DBK across to last st., BK 1.
Row 9 . . . Lilac . . . DBK across to last st., BK 1.
Row 10 . . . Lilac . . . DP across to last st., P 1.
Row 11 . . . Lilac . . . DBK across to last st., BK 1.
Row 12 . . . Lilac . . . DP across to last st., P 1.
Row 13 . . . Black . . . DBK across to last st., BK 1.
Row 14 . . . Black . . . DBK across to last st., BK 1.
Row 15 . . . Skipper Blue . . . DBK across to last st., BK 1.
Row 16 . . . Skipper Blue . . . DP across to last st., P 1.
Row 17 . . . Skipper Blue . . . DBK across to last st., BK 1.
Row 18 . . . Skipper Blue . . . DP across to last st., P 1.
Row 19 . . . Black . . . DBK across to last st., BK 1.
Row 20 . . . Black . . . DBK across to last st., BK 1.
Row 21 . . . Emerald . . . DBK across to last st., BK 1.

41

Row 22 . . . Emerald . . . DP across to last st., P 1.
Row 23 . . . Emerald . . . DBK across to last st., BK 1.
Row 24 . . . Emerald . . . DP across to last st., P 1.
Row 25 . . . Black . . . DBK across to last st., BK 1.
Row 26 . . . Black . . . DBK across to last st., BK 1.
Row 27 . . . Mid-Orange . . . DBK across to last st., BK 1.
Row 28 . . . Mid-Orange . . . DP across to last st., P 1.
Row 29 . . . Mid-Orange . . . DBK across to last st., BK 1.
Row 30 . . . Mid-Orange . . . DP across to last st., P 1.
Row 31 . . . Black . . . DBK across to last st., BK 1.
Row 32 . . . Black . . . DBK across to last st., BK 1.
Row 33 . . . Canary Yellow . . . DBK across to last st., BK 1.
Row 34 . . . Canary Yellow . . . DP across to last st., P 1.
Row 35 . . . Canary Yellow . . . DBK across to last st., BK 1.
Row 36 . . . Canary Yellow . . . DP across to last st., P 1.
Repeat the above 36 rows 6 times more—a total of 252 rows worked.
Row 253 . . . Black . . . DBK across to last st., BK 1.
Row 254 . . . Black . . . Bind-off repeating row 253.
FINISHING: Crochet Black sc edge along both sides. Fringe with 6″ black fringe across each end. Block.

LUMBERJACK CAP

MATERIAL: 2—4 oz. Skeins 4-Ply Knitted Worsted—1—
                Color A and 1—Color B
                1 pr. #15 Needles
GAUGE: 4 sts = 1″   7 rows = 2″
Using one strand of each color—Double Knit-On 48 sts.
PATTERN: Braid
Row 1 . . . DBK across to last st., BK 1.
Repeat Row 1 for a total of 80 rows or until piece measures the length of head measurement. This pattern was figured as a 22″ head measurement.
Bind-off Pattern: DBK 3, pass 1 st over 2 sts., *DBK 1, pass 1 st over 2 sts*, repeat from * to * to end of row.
FINISHING: Sew knit-on edge and bind-off edges together. Gather one end together tightly. Make a large pom-

pom out of the darker of the two colors and fasten over the gathered circle. Work yarn ends into back of work. No blocking necessary.

CABLE SCARF

MATERIAL: 2-2oz Skeins Wool 2-Ply Sports Yarn
                    1 pr. #15 Needles
GAUGE: 6 sts = 1″   7 rows = 2″
Double Knit-On 48 sts.
Row 1 . . . DBK across to last st., BK 1.
Row 2 . . . DP across to last st., P 1.
Row 3 . . . Repeat Row 1.
Row 4 . . . Repeat Row 2.
Row 5 . . . DBK 10, P 1, DBK 8, P 1, DBK 8, P 1, DBK 8, P 1, DBK 9, BK 1.
Row 6 . . . DP 10, K 1, DP 8, K 1, DP 8, K1, DP 8, K 1, DP 9, P 1.
Row 7 . . . Repeat Row 5.
Row 8 . . . Repeat Row 6.

43

Row 9 . . . Cable Row . . . DBK 10, P 1, *Remove 4 sts &
hold in front of work, transfer next 4 sts from
left needle to right needle, replace the 4 sts
held in front of work onto left needle, transfer
the 4 sts placed on right needle over to left
needle, DBK 8*, P 1, DBK 8, P 1, repeat from *
to *, P 1, DBK 9, BK 1.
Row 10 . . . Repeat Row 6.
Row 11 . . . Repeat Row 5.

Row 12 . . . Repeat Row 6.

Row 13 . . . Repeat Row 5.

Row 14 . . . Repeat Row 6.

Repeat Rows 9 thru 14—20 times more. There are now a total of 128 rows.

Rows 129 thru 132—Repeat Rows 9 thru 12.

Row 133 . . . Repeat Row 1.

Row 134 . . . Repeat Row 2.

Row 135 . . . Repeat Row 1.

BIND-OFF ON THE DOUBLE PURL SIDE using the following method. DP 3, Pass 1 st over 2 sts, *DP 1, Pass 1 st over 2 sts*, repeat from * to * to end of row, 2 sts remain on right needle, break yarn and pull thru the two sts.

FINISHING: Work beg and ending yarn ends into back side of work. Fringe across each end. Block.

QUICK CABLE SCARF
Approx. size 8″ x 60″

MATERIAL: 3—2 oz. Skeins Coats & Clark's Red Heart "Wintuk" Sport Yarn 2-Ply
1 pr. #17 Needles (½″)

GAUGE: 6 sts. = 1″   3 rows = 1″

Double Knit-On 50 sts.

Row 1 . . . DBK 4, P 1, DBK 10, P 1, DBK 3, P 1, DBK 10, P 1, DBK 3, P 1, DBK 10, P 1, DBK 3, BK 1.

Row 2 . . . DP 4, K 1, DP 10, K 1, DP 3, K 1, DP 10, K 1, DP 3, K 1, DP 10, K 1, DP 3, P 1.

Row 3 . . . Cable Row . . . DBK 4, P 1, *Remove 5 sts & Hold in back of work, transfer next 5 sts to right needle, replace the 5 sts in back on left needle and transfer the 5 sts placed on right needle over to left needle (this forms the twist in the cable), DBK 10, P 1, DBK 3, P 1*, repeat from * to * across the row working the last st as a BK 1 instead of P 1.

Row 4 . . . Repeat Row 2.

Row 5 . . . Repeat Row 1.

Row 6 . . . Repeat Row 2.

Continue to repeat Rows 3 thru 6 until the scarf measures 60″. Bind-off on Row 6 of the last repeat of pattern.
FINISHING: Fringe across both ends with 5″ fringe. Block.

OPEN LACE HOOD SCARF
Approx. size 8″ x 60″

MATERIAL: 4—2 oz. Skeins Coats & Clark's Red Heart Pompadour
1 pr. #17 Needles (½″)
GAUGE: 5 sts = 1″   2 rows = 1″
Double Knit-On 81 sts.

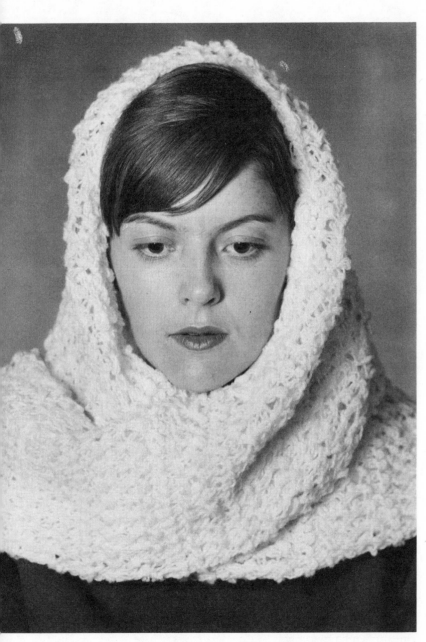

PATTERN: (Multiple of 3)

Row 1 ... DBK across to last st., BK 1.

Row 2 ... K2togBF across the row.

Row 3 ... DBK across to last st., BK 1.

Row 4 ... K3togBFB across the row.

Row 5 ... K3togFBF across the row.

Row 6 ... DP across to last st., P 1.

Row 7 ... K3togFBF across the row.

Row 8 ... K3togBFB across the row.

Repeat the above eight rows until scarf measures approximately 60". Pull down gently on your work as you knit to properly elongate the stitches.

Bind-off while repeating Row 1.

FINISHING: Block scarf to 16" x 60" size. Line with a complimentary color of chiffon. Fold scarf in half lengthwise and blind stitch edges together from each end for a length of 20". Leave the middle 20" open to be used as a hood over the head if desired, or wear folded shut as a neck scarf.

Fringe each end with 5" fringe.

NOTE: This scarf may be left open—16" x 60"—fringed across each end and worn as a summer stole.

LACE SQUARES SCARF
Approx. size 9" x 42"

MATERIAL: 2—2 oz. Skeins Wool 2-Ply Sports Yarn

                 1 pr. #13 Needles

GAUGE: 11 sts = 2"   4 rows = 1"

Double Knit-On 50 sts. (Multiple of 2 pattern).

Row 1 ... DBK across to last st., BK 1.

Row 2 ... DP across to last st., P 1.

Row 3 ... Repeat Row 1.

Row 4 ... Repeat Row 2.

Row 5 ... Repeat Row 1.

Row 6 ... Repeat Row 2.

Row 7 ... DBK 8, K2togFB across to last 8 sts., DBK 7, BK 1.

Row 8 . . . DP 8, K2togFB across to last 8 sts., DP 7, P 1.
Rows 9, 11, 13, 15, 17, 19, 21, 23, 25, 27 & 29—Repeat Row 7.
Rows 10, 12, 14, 16, 18, 20, 22, 24, 26, 28 & 30—Repeat Row 8.
Rows 31 & 33—Repeat Row 1.
Rows 32 & 34—Repeat Row 2.
Repeat Rows 7 thru 34 four times more. A total of 5 lace squares have been completed.
Repeat Rows 1 & 2 once more and bind-off while doing

the last Row 2 repeat.
FINISHING: Fringe across each end. Block.

STRIPED POT HOLDER
7″ x 7″

MATERIAL: Coats & Clark's O.N.T. Rug Yarn—1 Skein
each of Sapphire Blue, Parakeet, Hunter's
Green, Amethyst.
1 pr. #11 Needles

GAUGE: 4 sts = 1″   4 rows = 1″

Double Knit-On 112 sts in Sapphire Blue.

NOTE: All instructions shown between two *'s are to be repeated to the end of that row.

Row 1 . . . S. Blue . . . *DP2tog, DP 24, DP2tog*.
Row 2 . . . S. Blue . . . *DBK2tog, DBK 22, DBK2tog*.
Row 3 . . . S. Blue . . . *DP2tog, DP 20, DP2tog*.
Row 4 . . . Green . . . *DBK2tog, DBK 18, DBK2tog*.
Row 5 . . . Green . . . *DP2tog, DP 16, DP2tog*.
Row 6 . . . Green . . . *DBK2tog, DBK 14, DBK2tog*.
Row 7 . . . Parakeet . . . *DP2tog, DP 12, DP2tog*.
Row 8 . . . Parakeet . . . *DBK2tog, DBK 10, DBK2tog*.
Row 9 . . . Parakeet . . . *DP2tog, DP 8, DP2tog*.
Row 10 . . . Amethyst . . . *DBK2tog, DBK 6, DBK2tog*.
Row 11 . . . Amethyst . . . *DP2tog, DP 4, DP2tog*.
Row 12 . . . Amethyst . . . *DBK2tog, DBK 2, DBK2tog*.
Row 13 . . . Amethyst . . . *DP2tog*.

FINISHING: Pull yarn through remaining loops on needle. Secure firmly on back of work. Sew seam from center to corner. Work in yarn ends. Block.

SQUARE POT HOLDER
7″ x 7″

MATERIAL: Coats & Clark's O.N.T. Rug Yarn—Set of
2—1 Skein
1 pr. #11 Needles

GAUGE: 4 sts = 1″   4 rows = 1″

Double Knit-On 112 sts.

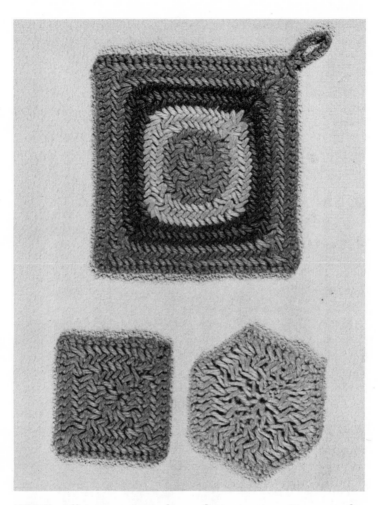

NOTE: All instructions shown between two *'s are to be repeated to the end of that row.

Row 1 . . . *DP2tog, DP 24, DP2tog*.

Row 2 . . . *DBK2tog, DBK 22, DBK2tog*.

Row 3 . . . *DP2tog, DP20, DP2tog*.

Row 4 . . . *DBK2tog, DBK 18, DBK2tog*.

Row 5 . . . *DP2tog, DP 16, DP2tog*.

Row 6 . . . *DBK2tog, DBK 14, DBK2tog*.

Row 7 . . . *DP2tog, DP 12, DP2tog*.
Row 8 . . . *DBK2tog, DBK 10, DBK2tog*.
Row 9 . . . *DP2tog, DP 8, DP2tog*.
Row 10 . . . *DBK2tog, DBK 6, DBK2tog*.
Row 11 . . . *DP2tog, DP 4, DP2tog*.
Row 12 . . . *DBK2tog, DBK 2, DBK2tog*.
Row 13 . . . *DP2tog*.
FINISHING: Pull yarn through remaining loops on needle. Secure firmly on back of work. Sew seam from center to corner. Work in yarn ends. Block.

SQUARE COASTER
3½″ x 3½″

MATERIAL: Coats & Clark's O.N.T. Rug Yarn—Set of 8—1 Skein
        1 pr. #11 Needles
GAUGE: 4 sts = 1″
Double Knit-On 56 sts.
NOTE: All instructions shown between two *'s are to be repeated to the end of that row.
Row 1 . . . *DP2tog, DP 10, DP2tog*.
Row 2 . . . *DBK2tog, DBK 8, DBK2tog*.
Row 3 . . . *DP2tog, DP 6, DP2tog*.
Row 4 . . . *DBK2tog, DBK 4, DBK2tog*.
Row 5 . . . *DP2tog, DP 2, DP2tog*.
Row 6 . . . *DBK2tog*.
FINISHING: Remove remaining stitches from needle and pull yarn thru securing it firmly on the back of the work. Sew seam from center to corner. Work in yarn ends on back. Block.

HEXAGON COASTER

MATERIAL: Coats & Clark's O.N.T. Rug Yarn—Set of 8—1 Skein
        1 pr. #13 Needles
GAUGE: 4 sts = 1″
Double Knit-On 60 sts.

NOTE: All instructions shown between two *'s are to be repeated to the end of that row.

Row 1 . . . *DP2tog, DP 6, DP2tog*.

Row 2 . . . *DBK2tog, DBK 4, DBK2tog*.

Row 3 . . . *DP2tog, DP 2, DP2tog*.

Row 4 . . . *DBK2tog*.

Row 5 . . . *DP2tog*.

FINISHING: Remove remaining 6 sts from needle. Break yarn and pull thru the stitches. Sew from center to corner. Secure yarn ends on back of work. Block.

HEXAGON HOT PAD

MATERIAL: 1 Skein each of Colors A, B, C, D—Coats & Clark's O.N.T. Rug Yarn
1—#11 Circular Needle (to be used as a straight needle)

GAUGE: 4 sts = 1″   4 rows = 1″
Double Knit-On 144 sts.

NOTE: All instructions shown between two *'s are to be repeated to the end of that row.

Row 1 . . . Color A . . . *DP2tog, DP 20, DP2tog*.

Row 2 . . . Color A . . . *DFK2tog, DFK 18, DFK2tog*.

Row 3 . . . Color A . . . *DP2tog, DP 16, DP2tog*.

Row 4 . . . Color B . . . *DFK2tog, DFK 14, DFK2tog . . . change to Color C . . . DFK2tog, DFK 14, DFK2tog . . . change to Color D . . . DFK2tog, DFK 14, DFK2tog*.

Row 5 . . . Color D . . . *DP2tog, DP 12, DP2tog . . . change to Color C . . . DP2tog, DP 12, DP2tog . . . change to Color B . . . DP2tog, DP 12, DP2tog*.

Row 6 . . . Color B . . . *DFK2tog, DFK 10, DFK2tog . . . change to Color C . . . DFK2tog, DFK 10, DFK2tog . . . change to Color D . . . DFK2tog, DFK 10, DFK2tog*.

Row 7 . . . Color D . . . *DP2tog, DP 8, DP2tog . . . change to Color C . . . DP2tog, DP 8, DP2tog . . . change

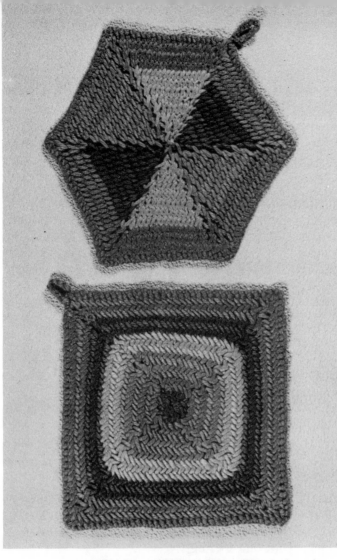

to Color B . . . DP2tog, DP 8, DP2tog*.

Row 8 . . . Color B . . . *DFK2tog, DFK 6, DFK2tog . . . change to Color C . . . DFK2tog, DFK 6, DFK2tog . . . change to Color D . . . DFK2tog, DFK 6, DFK2tog*.

Row 9 . . . Color D . . . *DP2tog, DP 4, DP2tog . . . change to Color C . . . DP2tog, DP 4, DP2tog . . . change to Color B . . . DP2tog, DP 4, DP2tog*.

Row 10 . . . Color B . . . *DFK2tog, DFK 2, DFK2tog . . .

change to Color C ... DFK2tog, DFK 2,
DFK2tog ... change to Color D ... DFK2tog,
DFK 2, DFK2tog*.

Row 11 ... Color D ... *DP2tog, DP2tog ... change to Col-
or C ... DP2tog, DP2tog ... change to Color B
... DP2tog, DP2tog*.

Row 12 ... Color B ... *DFK2tog, change to Color C ...
DFK2tog ... change to Color D ... DFK2tog*.

FINISHING: Pull yarn through remaining loops on the
needle. Secure firmly in back of work. Sew Seam from
corner to center. Work in yarn ends on back. Block.

HOT PAD
9″ x 9″

MATERIAL: Coats & Clark's O.N.T. Rug Yarn - 1 Skein
1 pr. #11 Needles

GAUGE: 4 sts = 1″   4 rows = 1″

Double Knit-On 144 sts.

NOTE: All instructions shown between two *'s are to be
repeated to the end of that row.

Row 1 ... *DP2tog, DP 32, DP2tog*.

Row 2 ... *DBK2tog, DBK 30, DBK2tog*.

Row 3 ... *DP2tog, DP 28, DP2tog*.

Row 4 ... *DBK2tog, DBK 26, DBK2tog*.

Row 5 ... *DP2tog, DP 24, DP2tog*.

Row 6 ... *DBK2tog, DBK 22, DBK2tog*.

Row 7 ... *DP2tog, DP 20, DP2tog*.

Row 8 ... *DBK2tog, DBK 18, DBK2tog*.

Row 9 ... *DP2tog, DP 16, DP2tog*.

Row 10 .. *DBK2tog, DBK 14, DBK2tog*.

Row 11 .. *DP2tog, DP 12, DP2tog*.

Row 12 .. *DBK2tog, DBK 10, DBK2tog*.

Row 13 .. *DP2tog, DP 8, DP2tog*.

Row 14 .. *DBK2tog, DBK 6, DBK2tog*.

Row 15 .. *DP2tog, DP 4, DP2tog*.

Row 16 .. *DBK2tog, DBK 2, DBK2tog*.

Row 17 .. *DP2tog*.

FINISHING: Pull yarn through remaining loops on the needle. Secure firmly in back of work. Sew seam from corner to center. Work in yarn ends on back. Block.

MULTI-STRIPED HOT PAD
9″ x 9″

The Multi-striped hot pad is worked the same as the regular 9″ x 9″ Hot Pad with the following exceptions:
Six Colors—Double Knit-On with Color 1.
Rows 1, 2, 3,—Color 1.
Rows 4, 5, 6,—Color 2.
Rows 7, 8, 9,—Color 3.
Rows 10, 11, 12—Color 4.
Rows 13, 14, 15—Color 5.
Rows 16, 17—Color 6.
Four Color Hot Pad—
Double Knit-On with Color 1.
Rows 1 - 4 . . . Color 1
Rows 5 - 8 . . . Color 2
Rows 9 - 12 . . . Color 3
Rows 13 - 17 . . . Color 4

PLACEMAT
11″ x 17″ Approx.

MATERIAL: Coats & Clark's O.N.T. Rug Yarn - Set of 6 Mats -
6 - Sapphire Blue, 4 - Hunter's Green, 5 - Parakeet, 3 - Amethyst
1 - 36″ Circular Needle #11

GAUGE: 4 sts = 1″   4 rows = 1″
Double Knit-On 224 sts in Sapphire Blue.
All instructions shown between two *'s are to be repeated to the end of that row.
Row 1 . . . Blue . . . *DP2tog, DP 40, DP2tog, DP2tog, DP 64, DP2tog*.
Row 2 . . . Blue . . . *DBK2tog, DBK 62, DBK2tog, DBK2tog, DBK 38, DBK2tog*.

56

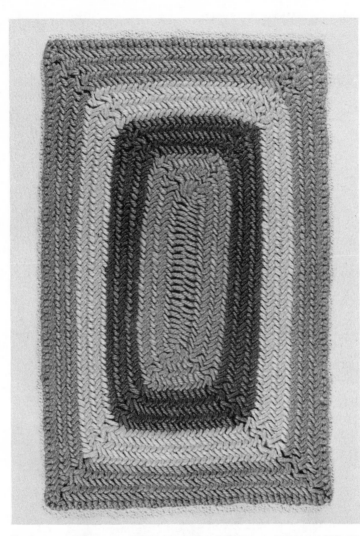

Row 3 . . . Blue . . . *DP2tog, DP 36, DP2tog, DP2tog, DP 60, DP2tog*.

Row 4 . . . Blue . . . *DBK2tog, DBK 58, DBK2tog, DBK2tog, DBK 34, DBK2tog*.

Row 5 . . . Blue . . . *DP2tog, DP 32, DP2tog, DP2tog, DP 56, DP2tog*.

Row 6 ... Parakeet ... *DBK2tog, DBK 54, DBK2tog, DBK 2tog, DBK 30, DBK2tog*.

Row 7 ... Parakeet ... *DP2tog, DP 28, DP2tog, DP2tog, DP 52, DP2tog*.

Row 8 ... Parakeet ... *DBK2tog, DBK 50, DBK2tog, DBK2 tog, DBK 26, DBK2tog*.

Row 9 ... Parakeet ... *DP2tog, DP 24, DP2tog, DP2tog, DP 48, DP2tog*.

Row 10 .. Parakeet ... *DBK2tog, DBK 46, DBK2tog, DBK 2tog, DBK 22, DBK2tog*.

Row 11 .. Green ... *DP2tog, DP 20, DP2tog, DP2tog, DP 44, DP2tog*.

Row 12 .. Green ... *DBK2tog, DBK 42, DBK2tog, DBK2 tog, DBK 18, DBK2tog*.

Row 13 .. Green ... *DP2tog, DP 16, DP2tog, DP2tog, DP 40, DP2tog*.

Row 14 .. Green ... *DBK2tog, DBK 38, DBK2tog, DBK2 tog, DBK 14, DBK2tog*.

Row 15 .. Green ... *DP2tog, DP 12, DP2tog, DP2tog, DP 36, DP2tog*.

Row 16 .. Amethyst ... *DBK2tog, DBK 34, DBK2tog, DBK 2tog, DBK 10, DBK2tog*.

Row 17 .. Amethyst ... *DP2tog, DP 8, DP2tog, DP2tog, DP 32, DP2tog*.

Row 18 .. Amethyst ... *DBK2tog, DBK 30, DBK2tog, DBK 2tog, DBK 6, DBK2tog*.

Row 19 .. Amethyst ... *DP2tog, DP 4, DP2tog, DP2tog, DP 28, DP2tog*.

Row 20 .. Amethyst ... *DBK2tog, DBK 26, DBK2tog, DBK 2tog, DBK 2, DBK2tog*.

Row 21 .. Amethyst ... *DP2tog, DP2tog, DP2tog, DP 24, DP2tog*.

FINISHING: Remove all stitches from needle. Place knitted placemat in a rectangular shape. Weave the 24 stitches opposite each other in the center together. Draw the yarn end thru the two end stitches. Weave seam from center to corner. Work in all yarn ends on the back of the work. Block.

TABLE RUNNER
11″ x 34″

MATERIAL: Coats & Clark's O.N.T. Rug Yarn - 2 - Sapphire Blue, 2 - Parakeet, 1 - Hunter's Green & 1 - Amethyst

1 - 36″ Circular Needle #11

GAUGE: 4 sts = 1″   4 rows = 1″

Double Knit-On 360 sts using the Sapphire Blue.

NOTE: All instructions shown between two *'s are to be repeated to the end of that row.

Row 1 . . . Blue . . . *DP2tog, DP 40, DP2tog, DP2tog, DP 132, DP2tog*.

Row 2 . . . Blue . . . *DBK2tog, DBK 130, DBK2tog, DBK2 tog, DBK 38, DBK2tog*.

Row 3 . . . Blue . . . *DP2tog, DP 36, DP2tog, DP2tog, DP 128 DP2tog*.

Row 4 . . . Blue . . . *DBK2tog, DBK 126, DBK2tog, DBK2 tog, DBK 34, DBK2tog*.

Row 5 . . . Blue . . . *DP2tog, DP 36, DP2tog, DP2tog, DP 124, DP2tog*.

Row 6 . . . Parakeet . . . *DBK2tog, DBK 122, DBK2tog, DBK 2tog, DBK 30, DBK2tog*.

Row 7 . . . Parakeet . . . *DP2tog, DP 28, DP2tog, DP2tog, DP 120, DP2tog*.

Row 8 . . . Parakeet . . . *DBK2tog, DBK 118, DBK2tog, DBK 2tog, DBK 26, DBK2tog*.

Row 9 . . . Parakeet . . . *DP2tog, DP 24, DP2tog, DP2tog, DP 116, DP2tog*.

Row 10 . . Parakeet . . . *DBK2tog, DBK 114, DBK2tog, DBK 2tog, DBK 22, DBK2tog*.

Row 11 . . Green . . . *DP2tog, DP 20, DP2tog, DP2tog, DP 112, DP2tog*.

Row 12 . . Green . . . *DBK2tog, DBK 110, DBK2tog, DBK2 tog, DBK 18, DBK2tog*.

Row 13 . . Green . . . *DP2tog, DP 16, DP2tog, DP2tog, DP 108, DP2tog*.

Row 14 . . Green . . . *DBK2tog, DBK 106, DBK2tog, DBK2 tog, DBK 14, DBK2tog*.

Row 15 . . Green . . . *DP2tog, DP 12, DP2tog, DP2tog, DP 104, DP2tog*.

Row 16 . . Amethyst . . . *DBK2tog, DBK 102, DBK2tog, DBK2tog, DBK 10, DBK2tog*.

Row 17 . . Amethyst . . . *DP2tog, DP 8, DP2tog, DP2tog, DP 100, DP2tog*.

Row 18 . . Amethyst . . . *DBK2tog, DBK 98, DBK2tog, DBK

2tog, DBK 6, DBK2tog*.

Row 19 .. Amethyst . . . *DP2tog, DP 4, DP2tog, DP2tog, DP 96, DP2tog*.

Row 20 .. Amethyst . . . *DBK2tog, DBK 94, DBK2tog, DBK 2tog, DBK 2, DBK2tog*.

Row 21 .. Amethyst . . . *DP2tog, DP2tog, DP2tog, DP 92, DP2tog*.

FINISHING: Remove all stitches from needle. Place knitted table runner in a rectangular shape. Weave the 92 stitches opposite each other in the center together. Draw the yarn end thru the two end stitches. Weave seam from center to corner. Work in all yarn ends on the back of the work. Block.

STAINED GLASS BEDSPREAD
Twin Size

MATERIAL: Coats & Clark's Red Heart Knitted Worsted 4-Ply - 1-4 oz. Skein for each 2 rectangles. Total of 52 rectangles.

12 - Purple	. . . . .6 Skeins
10 - Orange	. . . . .5 Skeins
9 - Yellow	. . . . .5 Skeins
7 - Green	. . . . .4 Skeins
7 - Blue	. . . . . .4 Skeins
7 - Red	. . . . . . .4 Skeins

4 Skeins - Black for fringe & crochet.

1 pr. #13 Needles   1 - Size G Crochet Hook

GAUGE: 6 sts = 1″   7 rows = 2″

Directions are for one rectangular piece. Size 8″ x 16″.

Double Knit-On 48 sts.

Row 1 . . . DBK across to last st., BK 1.

Row 2 . . . DP across to last st., P 1.

Repeat rows 1 & 2 until piece measures 15½″.

Bind-off in pattern.

FINISHING: Single crochet around each rectangle with black. Block each one to the 8″ x 16″ size. Follow diagram for color arrangement and slip stitch the rectangles togeth-

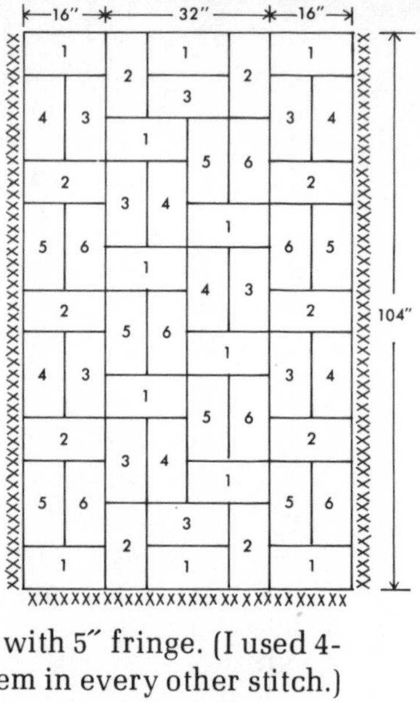

COLOR CODE:

1 - Lilac   4 - Green
2 - Orange   5 - Blue
3 - Yellow   6 - Red
     X - Black Fringe

Twin Bed .... 64″ x 104″
                     without fringe
Full Bed .... 96″ x 104″
                     without fringe
King Bed .... 112″ x 104″
                     without fringe

er with black. Fringe quite heavily with 5″ fringe. (I used 4-11″ pieces for fringe and placed them in every other stitch.) Do not fringe across the top.

NOTE: For a full-size bedspread, repeat the squares in

62

the first 16″ of each side. Leave the center squares as they are.

King size: Repeat the center 32″, leaving the 16″ borders as shown in the diagram. Separate the center 32″ strips with a 16″ strip of border. This gives you 16″ border strip, 32″ center strip, 16″ border strip, 32″ center strip, 16″ border strip.

BOLERO VEST

MATERIAL: Reynold's Patte de Velours - 6 Skeins
1 pr. #11 Needles

GAUGE: 5 sts = 1″   4 rows = 1″

Using a double strand of yarn . . .

Double Knit-On 70 sts (bottom of the back).

Row 1 . . . DBK across to last st., BK 1.

Row 2 . . . DP2tog, DP across to last 2 sts., P2tog.

Rows 3 - 6 . . . Repeat Rows 1 & 2.

Row 7 . . . DBK Across to last st., BK 1.

Row 8 . . . DP across to last st., P 1.

Rows 9 - 28 . . . Repeat Rows 7 & 8.

Row 29 . . DBK across to last 5 sts., TURN.

Row 30 . . Sl 1, DP across to last 5 sts., TURN.

Row 31 . . Sl 1, DBK across to last 10 sts., TURN.

Row 32 . . Sl 1, DP across to last 10 sts., TURN.

Row 33 . . Sl 1, DBK 5, Bind-off 32, DBK 6, Sl 1, TURN.

Begin Left Front . . .

Row 34 . . DP across to last st., P 1.

Row 35 . . DBK 11, Sl 1, TURN.

Row 36 . . DP across to last st., P 1.

Row 37 . . DBK across to last st., BK 1.

Row 38 . . DP across to last st., P 1.

Row 39 . . Inc 1 in 1st st by DBK-ing the first st and instead of removing the worked st., slip it to the right needle, Continue to DBK across to last st., BK 1.

Row 40 . . DP across to last st., P 1.

Repeat rows 39 and 40 until a total of 63 rows have been worked ending with the DBK row.

Row 64 . . Inc 1 st at beg of row, DP across to last st., P 1.

Row 65 . . Repeat row 39.

Row 66 . . Repeat row 64.

Row 67 . . Repeat row 39.

Row 68 . . Repeat row 64.

Row 69 . . Bind-off in DBK.

Begin Right Front . . . Attach yarn at neck edge, continuing over the shoulder and down the right front . . .

Row 34 . . DP 6, Sl 1, TURN.

Row 35 . . DBK across to last st., BK 1.

Row 36 . . DP 11, Sl 1, TURN.

Row 37 . . DBK across to last st., BK 1.

Row 38 . . DP across to last st., P 1.

Row 39 . . DBK across to last st., DBK 1.

Row 40 . . Inc 1 st in 1st st by DP-ing thru the first st., and slipping the worked st to the right needle instead of removing it, continue to DP across to last st., P 1.

Row 41 . . DBK across to last st., BK 1.

Repeat Rows 40 & 41 until a total of 64 rows have been worked ending with a DP row.

Row 65 . . Inc 1 st at beg of row, DBK across to last st., BK 1.

Row 66 . . Repeat Row 40.

Row 67 . . Repeat Row 65.

Row 68 . . Repeat Row 40.

Row 69 . . Repeat Row 65.

Row 70 . . Bind-off in DP.

FINISHING: Attach yarn at underarm front and crochet a double chain of 10 sts and attach to underarm back. Repeat the same on the opposite side. Using two 48″ strands of yarn, fringe in every other stitch across both fronts and the back. Do not fringe on the underarm chain. Block. Steam the fringe so that it hangs straight.

ALL-PURPOSE SQUARE

MATERIAL: 1 - 4 oz. Skein Germantown Knitted Worsted 4-Ply per 2 squares - Blocked Size 13″ x 13″

1 pr. #13 Needles

COLOR CODE:
A - Pink
B - Red
X - Pink & Red Fringe
Large X's denote feather
stitching

GAUGE: 5 sts = 1″   7 rows = 2″

Double Knit-On 66 sts.

Row 1 . . . DP across to last st., P 1.

Row 2 . . . DFK across to last st., K 1.

Row 3 . . . Repeat Row 1.

Row 4 . . . Repeat Row 2.

Row 5 . . . Repeat Row 1.

66

Row 6 . . . DFK 8, *K2togFB*, repeat from * to * across to
           last 8 sts., DFK 7, K 1.

Row 7 . . . DP across to last st., P 1.

Rows 8 - 41 . . . Repeat rows 6 & 7.

Row 42 . . DFK across to last st., K 1.

Row 43 . . DP across to last st., P 1.

Row 44 . . Repeat Row 42.

Row 45 . . Repeat Row 43.

Row 46 . . Bind-off while repeating Row 42.

FINISHING: Block to size. Work in yarn ends.

ALL-PURPOSE SQUARE PONCHO

MATERIAL: Germantown Knitted Worsted - 4-Ply - 1 -
               4 oz. Skein Color A - 1 - 4 oz. Skein Color B
               1 pr. #13 Needles

GAUGE: 5 sts = 1″   7 rows = 2″

Knit 2 squares of Color A and 2 squares of Color B following directions for the All Purpose Square. Block the 4
squares. Following the diagram, feather stitch the four
squares together. The arrow indicates the side of the 1st
square of Color A that is to be feather stitched to the side
of the last square of Color B.

Using 4 strands for each fringe, alternate Color A and
Color B fringe all the way around the outside edge. 11″
strands are required for 5″ fringe. Slip stitch around the
neck edge with Color B.

PILLOW COVER
13″ x 13″

MATERIAL: 1 - 4 oz. Skein Germantown Knitted Wor-
               sted - 4-Ply
               1 pr. #13 Needles

GAUGE: 5 sts = 1″   7 rows = 2″

Knit two squares following the directions for the All Purpose Square.

FINISHING METHOD #1: With reverse sides of squares
facing each other, single crochet the edges together on

three sides. Stuff with a foam rubber pillow form of the proper size and single crochet the fourth side closed. Make 4 tassels—each using 24 - 8″ strands of yarn. Attach one tassel to each corner of the pillow.

FINISHING METHOD #2: Cut 244 - 8″ lengths of yarn— place the reverse sides of the squares together and fringe around three sides. Stuff pillow and close fourth side by fringing it together.

PILLOW COVER
17″ x 17″

MATERIAL: 2 - 4 oz. Skeins Germantown Knitted Worsted - 4-Ply
1 pr. #13 Needles

GAUGE: 5 sts = 1″   7 rows = 2″

Knit 4 squares following the directions for the All Purpose Square.

FINISHING: Sew the four squares together placed side by side out flat. Fold one half (two squares) over the other half and sew the ends together. Take the top and bottom of the side remaining open and bring them together in the center. This places the open seam in a corner to corner position and brings the four squares into a triangular position on each side. Slip stitch the one remaining seam closed. Make 4 large tassels, one for each corner. If desired, cover a large button for each side—attaching one to center front and one to center back and draw the connecting threads tightly.

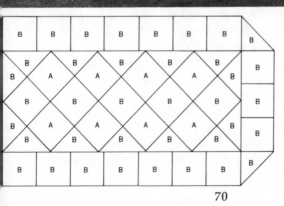

70

ALL-PURPOSE SQUARE BEDSPREAD

MATERIAL: Germantown Knitted Worsted 4-Ply - Color A - 4 - 4 oz. Skeins, Color B - 15 - 4 oz. Skeins

1 pr. #13 Needles

GAUGE: 5 sts = 1″   7 rows = 2″

With Color A—Knit 8 All Purpose Squares.

With Color B—Knit 30 All Purpose Squares.

FINISHING: Block each square individually. Follow the diagram for placement of the colors and machine stitch together allowing a ¼″ seam. The half squares are from squares that have been cut in half from corner to corner. Unless you are really good at putting things together, I would suggest that you put a double line of machine stitching from corner to corner and cut in between the stitching. This prevents any give whatsoever to the knit. It is well to remember that the center of the all purpose square is a design stitch that is worked twice, but is not one of the basic three stitches which will not run or unravel.

NOTE: This makes a youth bed size spread or coverlet for a twin bed to be used with a dust ruffle. Should a wider spread be desired, add another row of Color B squares along each side and across the end.

BIKINI

MATERIAL: 4 oz. Phentex

1 pr. #13 Needles

1 yd. ½″ Elastic

GAUGE: 5 sts = 1″   7 rows = 2″

The bikini bottoms are knitted in one piece beginning at the top edge across the back. Directions are for size 10 (12, 14).

Double Knit-On 80 (85, 90) sts.

Row 1 . . . DBK across to last st., BK 1.

Row 2 . . . DP across to last st., P 1.

Row 3 . . . DFK 2, *Y.O., DFK2tog*, repeat from * to * across to last two sts., DFK 1, K 1.

Row 4 . . . DP 2, *Y.O., DP2tog*, repeat from * to * across to last two sts., DP 1, P 1.

Repeat Rows 3 & 4 until a total of 10 rows have been worked.

Size 12 . . . Repeat Rows 3 & 4 once more.

Size 14 . . . Repeat Rows 3 & 4 twice more.

Row 11 . . . DBK2tog (Drop 1, Sl 1), DBK2tog, DBK2tog, DBK across to last 5 sts., DBK2tog, DBK2tog, Sl 1.

Row 12 . . . DP2tog (Drop 1, Sl 1), DP2tog, DP2tog, DP across to last 5 sts., DP2tog, DP2tog, Sl 1.

Row 13 . . . Repeat Row 11.

Row 14 . . . Repeat Row 12.

Row 15 . . . DBK2tog(Drop 1, Sl 1), DBK2tog, DBK across to last 3 sts., DBK2tog, Sl 1.

72

Row 16 . . . DP2tog(Drop 1, Sl 1), DP2tog, DP across to last 3 sts., DP2tog, Sl 1.

Rows 17 - 34 . . . Repeat Rows 15 & 16.

Size 12 . . . Repeat Rows 15 & 16 once more.

Size 14 . . . Repeat Rows 15 & 16 twice more.

Crotch

Rows 35 - 48 . . . Repeat Rows 1 & 2.

Size 12 . . . Repeat Rows 1 & 2 once more.

Size 14 . . . Repeat Rows 1 & 2 twice more.

Row 49 . . . DBK2tog(Drop 1, Sl 1), Inc. 1 in each of the next two DBK sts., DBK across to the last 4 sts., Inc 1 in each of the next two DBK sts., DBK 1, Sl 1.

Row 50 . . . DP2tog(Drop 1, Sl 1), Inc. 1 in each of the next 2 DP sts., DP across to the last 4 sts., Inc 1 in each of the next 2 DP sts., DP 1, Sl 1.

Row 51 . . . DBK2tog(Drop 1, Sl 1), Inc 1 in the next DBK st., DBK across to the last 3 sts., Inc 1 in the next DBK st., DBK 1, Sl 1.

Row 52 . . . DP2tog(Drop 1, Sl 1), Inc 1 in the next DP st., DP across to the last 3 sts., Inc 1 in the next DP st., DP 1, Sl 1.

Row 53 . . . Repeat Row 51.

Row 54 . . . Repeat Row 52.

Row 55 . . . Repeat Row 51.

Size 12 . . . Repeat Rows 52 & 51 once more.

Size 14 . . . Repeat Rows 52 & 51 twice more.

Row 56 . . . Double Knit-On 17 sts., DP across the row. Double Knit-On 18 sts.

Row 57 . . . DBK across to last st., BK 1.

Row 58 . . . DP 2, *Y.O., DP2tog*, repeat from * to * across to last two sts., DP 1, Sl 1.

Row 59 . . . DFK 2, *Y.O., DFK2tog*, repeat from * to * across to last two sts., DFK 1, Sl 1.

Row 60 . . . Repeat Row 58.

Row 61 . . . Repeat Row 59.

Row 62 . . . Repeat Row 58.

Row 63 . . . Repeat Row 59.

(Size 12 . . . Repeat Rows 58 & 59 once more.)

73

(Size 14 . . . Repeat Rows 58 & 59 twice more.)

Row 64 . . . DP across to last st., P 1.

Row 65 . . . Bind-off in DBK.

FINISHING: Sew the even side edges together (the lace sections). Measure the length of elastic required to go around hips comfortably and sew the ends together. Place the elastic inside around the top and stitch it in place by picking up one stitch at the top of the elastic and then one stitch at the bottom of the elastic as per illustration for doing waistbands.

BRA TOP:

Directions are for Bra Cup Size B (C, D). Knit two squares.

Double Knit-On 30 (36, 40) sts.

Row 1 . . . DBK across to last st., BK 1.

Row 2 . . . DP across to last st., P 1.

Rows 3 - 12 . . . Repeat Rows 1 & 2.

(Size C . . . Repeat Rows 1 & 2 once more.)

(Size D . . . Repeat Rows 1 & 2 twice more.)

Row 13 . . . DFK 2; *Y.O., DFK2tog*, repeat from * to * to last two sts., DFK 1, Sl 1.

Row 14 . . . DP 2, *Y.O., DP2tog*, repeat from * to * to last two sts., DP 1, Sl 1.

Rows 15 - 18 . . . Repeat Rows 13 & 14.

(Size C . . . Repeat Rows 13 & 14 once more.)

(Size D . . . Repeat Rows 13 & 14 twice more.)

Row 19 . . . Bind-off in DBK.

FINISHING: See illustration showing dart placement in the bra cup. Each corner of the square is labeled. The bind-off edge is labeled corner A and corner B, while the knit-on edge is labeled C & D. Take Corner D and fold it over to meet Corner C. On the reverse side of the work,

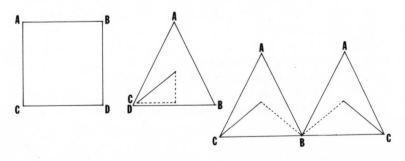

sew a dart from the center of the square to the corner which is now CD. If desired, the dart may be cut open so that the triangle can be placed along the inside of the bottom of the bra cup for extra support. This also relieves any bulk from the dart. The two cups have the dart placed to opposite corners—thus, for the left bra cup, corner C would be folded over to Corner D and the dart sewed from the center of the square. Now, place the squares side-by-side as shown in the illustration. Crochet around the entire outside edge. Crochet double chains of the length desired from the point corner A and from the points at corner C. The chain from C is to be tied around the back. The chain from A is to be tied around the neck or made to come down to meet the back straps.

BASIC SHELL

MATERIAL: 6 - 2 oz. Skeins Coats & Clark's Red Heart Pompadour
                    1 pr. #11 needles   1 Size H crochet hook
                    1 - 6″ neck opening zipper or 2 small buttons

GAUGE: 8 sts = 1″   4 rows = 1″

NOTE: Directions are for size 10. Changes for sizes 12, 14, 16 and 18 are in parentheses.

BLOCKING MEASUREMENTS: Bust - 34(35, 37, 39, 41)″; width of back or front at underarms - 17(17½, 18½, 19½, 20½)″; length from hemline to underarms - 12½″; length from hemline to back of neck - 21(21, 21½, 21½, 22)″.

PATTERN: Herringbone

Row 1 . . . DBK across to last st., BK 1.

Row 2 . . . DP across to last st., P 1.

NOTE: Pull down gently on your work as you knit to properly elongate the stitch before measuring each time.

BACK: Double Knit-On 136(140, 148, 156, 164) sts.

Work in Herringbone stitch for 1″ ending with a DP row. DP next row on right side for hemline. Beginning with a

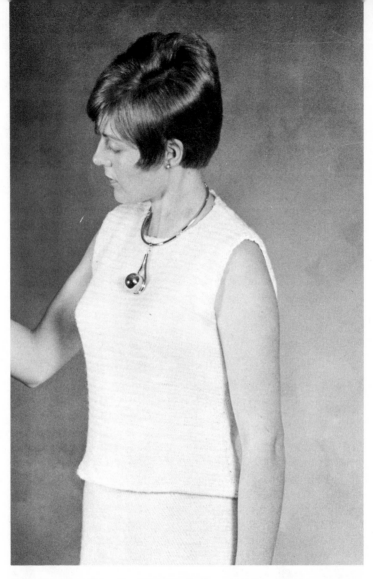

DP row, continue in Herringbone st until piece measures 12½ ″ *above hemline* (or desired length to underarms) ending with a DP row. Mark last row.

ARMHOLES: Bind-off 6 sts at beg of next 2 rows. Dec 2 sts *each side* every DBK row 3(3, 4, 5, 6) times. Work even on 112(112, 116, 120, 124) sts until armholes measure 2(2, 2½, 2½, 3)″ above marked row, ending with DBK row.

DIVIDE FOR BACK OPENING: DP 56(56, 58, 60, 62) sts, tie in another ball of yarn, DP last 56(56, 58, 60, 62) sts. Continue working on each side with a separate ball of yarn, or work 1 side at a time if you prefer. Work even until armholes measure 7½(7½, 8, 8, 8½)″ above marked row.

SHOULDERS: Bind-off 12 sts from each armhole edge every other row twice, then 10(12, 12, 14, 14) sts once. Bind off 22(22, 24, 24, 26) sts on each side.

FRONT: Work same as back (omitting back opening) until armholes measure 5 (5, 5½, 5½, 6)″ above marked row, ending with a DP row.

NECK: DBK 42(44, 46, 48, 50) sts, tie in another ball of yarn, bind-off center 28 sts, DBK to end. Continue working on each side with a separate ball of yarn, or work 1 side at a time if you prefer. Dec 2 sts at neck edge every row 4 (4, 5, 5, 6) times. Work even on 34(36, 36, 38, 38) sts until armholes measure 7½(7½, 8, 8, 8½)″.

SHOULDERS: Bind-off 12 sts from each armhole edge every other row twice, then 10(12, 12, 14, 14) sts once.

FINISHING: Block pieces to measurements. Sew underarm and shoulder seams. Turn hem to wrong side at hemline and slip stitch in place. From right side, work 1 row sc around neck edge, back opening and armholes, spacing sts to keep edges flat. Two more rows of sc around neck and armhole edge may be added if desired. Sew in zipper so it does not show. If buttons are preferred—chain st two loops—one at the top right back opening and one halfway between the top and bottom of the right back opening. Sew buttons on corresponding places on left back opening. Steam lightly the seams and edges.

LACE MAXI SCARF
Approx. size 8″ x 9′

MATERIAL: 4 - 4 oz. Skeins Coats & Clark's Red Heart 4-Ply Knitted Worsted.
1 pr. #17 Needles (½″)

GAUGE: 6 sts = 1″   2 rows = 1″

Double Knit-On 48 sts.
PATTERN: (Multiple of 2)
Row 1 . . . DFK across to last st., K 1.
Row 2 . . . K2togFB across the row.
Row 3 . . . DBK across to last st., BK 1.
Row 4 . . . K2togFB across the row.
Repeat the 4 rows of pattern until scarf measures 8′ in length. Pull down gently and frequently on your work to elongate the stitches properly.
Bind-off while repeating Row 1.
FINISHING: Fringe across each end with 5″ fringe. Block.

BASIC SKIRT

MATERIAL: 4—4 oz. Skeins Coats & Clark's Red Heart
              4-Ply Knitted Worsted
              1—#15 Circular Needle
              1 yd. ¾" Elastic

GAUGE: 6 sts = 1"   3 rows = 1"

NOTE: Directions are for size 10 with sizes 12, 14, 16 and 18 in parentheses.

Hip Measurements: 34 (36, 38, 40, 42)".

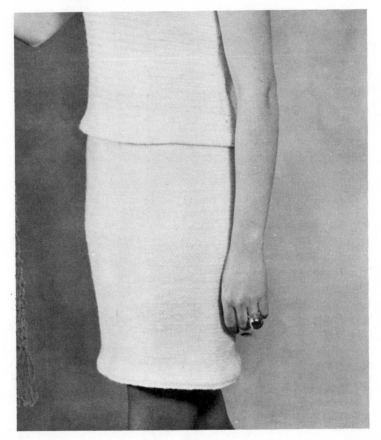

Double Knit-On 204 (216, 228, 240, 252) sts.
Place a marker at the beginning, making certain the knit-on edge is not twisted, slip the last st knit-on over by the first st on the other end. DBK thru these two sts to join the circle. Continue to DBK around the circle.
A hem is not necessary, but if desired, DBK three complete circles. DP one circle for the turning row of the hem.
If a hem is not desired, begin following directions at this point, omitting the paragraph concerning the hem.
DBK circles continually until the piece measures desired length.

MINISKIRT—Approx. 16″.
REGULAR SKIRT—Approx. 20″.
MIDI-SKIRT—Approx. 30″.
MAXI-SKIRT—Approx. 39″.

BAND: Triple Back Knit three complete circles. This is done by knitting thru 3 sts each time and still only removing 1 st. Thus you work thru each stitch three times and the band becomes nice and firm. BIND-OFF by passing 1 st over 3 sts.

FINISHING: Work in yarn ends. Cut elastic to fit waist comfortably and sew the ends together. Place inside waistband on the reverse and slip stitch over by taking a stitch from the top of the band and one from the bottom. See illustration.

ELASTIC WAISTBAND

Cut elastic to desired length for waist measurement. Sew ends together. Place the elastic inside the knitted waistband. With a darning needle and a length of yarn, slip stitch the elastic in place by going thru a stitch at the top of the waistband and then thru a stitch at the bottom of the waistband. Stitching thru every other stitch is adequate. Secure yarn ends when complete and work ends into back of work.

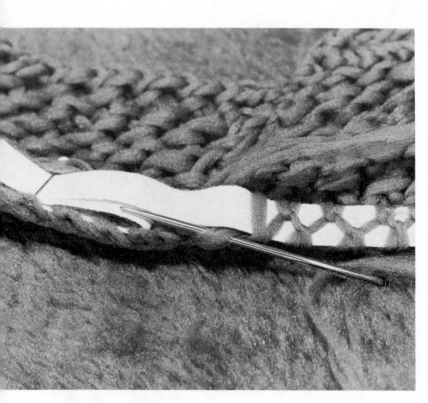

RUBAN SHELL

MATERIAL: 4 oz. Phentex Ruban
                    1 pr. #11 Needles
                    1 Size H Crochet Hook
                    2—Small Buttons

GAUGE: 15 sts = 2″   7 rows = 2″

NOTE: Directions are for size 5 with changes for sizes 7, 9, 11 and 13 in parentheses.

Pull down on your work as you knit to elongate the stitch properly, also before measuring each time.

PATTERN: Silhouette Stitch

Row 1 . . . DFK across to last st., K 1.

Row 2 . . . DP across to last st., P 1.

BACK: Double Knit-On 120 (124, 130, 138, 144) sts. Work

81

in Silhouette Stitch for 1″ ending with a DP row. DP next
row on right side for hemline. Beginning with a DP row,
continue in Silhouette St until piece measures 12½″
above hemline (or desired length to underarms) ending
with a DP row. Mark last row.

ARMHOLES: Bind-off 5 sts at beg of next 2 rows. Dec 2 sts
each side every DFK row 3 (3, 4, 5, 6) times. Work even on
98 (100, 104, 108, 110) sts until armholes measure 2 (2, 2½,

2½, 3)″ above marked row, ending with DFK row.

DIVIDE FOR BACK OPENING: DP 49 (50, 52, 54, 55) sts, tie in another ball of yarn, DP last 49 (50, 52, 54, 55) sts. Continue working on each side with a separate ball of yarn, or work 1 side at a time if you prefer. Work even until armholes measure 7½ (7½, 8, 8, 8½)″ above marked row.

SHOULDERS: Bind-off 11 sts from each armhole edge every other row twice, then 8 (9, 9, 11, 11) sts once. Bind-off remaining 19 (19, 21, 21, 22) sts on each side.

FRONT: Work same as back (omitting back opening) until armholes measure 5 (5, 5½, 5½, 6)″ above marked row, ending with a DP row.

NECK: DFK 37 (38, 40, 42, 43) sts, tie in another ball of yarn, bind-off center 24 sts, DFK to end. Continue working on each side with a separate ball of yarn, or work 1 side at a time if you prefer. Dec 2 sts at neck edge every row 4 (4, 5, 5, 6) times. Work even on 29 (30, 30, 32, 31) sts until armholes measure 7½ (7½, 8, 8, 8½)″.

SHOULDERS: Bind-off 10 sts from each armhole edge every other row twice, then 9 (10, 10, 12, 11) sts once.

FINISHING: Sew underarm and shoulder seams. Turn hem to wrong side at hemline and slip stitch in place. From right side, single crochet around neck edge, back opening and armholes, spacing sts to keep edges flat. Two more rows of sc around neck and armhole edge may be added if desired. Chain button loops on right side of back opening and sew buttons on corresponding positions on left side of back opening.

NOTE: If blocking is desired, RUBAN is blocked best by wetting each piece completely, pin to blocking measurement size, let dry completely before unpinning. *Do not use steam.*

BASIC SKIRT FOR JUNIORS

MATERIALS: 5—2 oz. Skeins Nylon Sports Yarn 2-Ply
1 Size 11 or 13 Needle
1 yd. ¾″ Elastic

GAUGE: 6 sts = 1″   #11 Needle—4 rows = 1″

                                     #13 Needle—7 rows = 2″

Take actual hip measurement and add 2″. Knits do not look their best if skin tight. Multiple the number of inches by 6. This will be the number of stitiches you double knit-on to begin the skirt.

Take the last stitch knit-on and slip it over to the first stitch on the other end of the needle. DBK thru these two stitches to join the circle. NOTE: Be certain the knit-on edge is not twisted *before* joining the circle.

Continue to knit circles in DBK until the piece measures 1″ less than the desired finished length.

Now, dec 1 st in every 10 or 12 sts. This is not a definite type of decrease—it just keeps the waistband from being too bulky.

WAISTBAND: TBK—triple back knit (knit thru three sts and drop off 1 each time) one inch of circles. Bind-off. Work in beg and ending yarn ends.

FINISHING: Cut elastic to fit waist comfortably. Sew ends together. Place the elastic inside the waistband and slip stitch it in place according to illustration on page 81.

SKIRT—SOFTLY GATHERED

MATERIAL: 6—50 gram Balls Scheepjes—Crylor

                        1 Size 15 Circular Needle

                        1 yd. ¾″ Elastic

GAUGE: 5 sts = 1″   3 rows = 1″

Take actual hip measurements and add 5 to 7 inches depending on amount of fullness desired in skirt. 5″ extra makes a nice soft skirt. Multiple the number of inches by 5. Double knit-on this number of stitches. Place the last stitch knit-on over by the first st on the opposite end of the needle (be sure the knit-on edge is not twisted). DBK thru these two stitches to secure the circle. Continue to DBK circles until the piece measures 1″ shorter than actual length desired. Dec 1 st in every 10th st throughout the next two circles knitted.

WAISTBAND: TBK—triple back knit (knit thru 3 sts and drop off 1 st each time) 3 complete circles. Bind-off by passing 1 st over 3 sts.

FINISHING: Work in yarn ends. Cut elastic to fit waist comfortably. Place elastic inside knitted waistband and slip stitch it in place by taking one stitch from the top of the band and then one stitch from the bottom of the band. Sewing thru every other stitch is sufficient.

No blocking necessary. Steam lightly for appearance if desired.

THE PONCHO

MATERIAL: Phentex—4—3.2 oz. Skeins Black
3—3.2 oz. Skeins Red
2—3.2 oz. Skeins White
1 Size #15 Circular Needle
1—24″ Jacket Zipper

GAUGE: 4 sts = 1″   3 rows = 1″

Double Knit-On using Black 120 sts (left front), place marker, 240 sts (back), place marker, 120 sts (right front). Total number of sts on needle—480.

Row 1 . . . Black—DBK across to last st., Sl 1.

Row 2 . . . Black—Repeat Row 1.

Row 3 . . . Black—Repeat Row 1.

Row 4 . . . Black—Repeat Row 1.

NOTE: At this point you decide whether you want to knit the first and fourth rows together as you knit the first row of red or if you want to slip stitch them together by hand after. Either way works great.

Row 5 . . .   Red—DBK across to last st, dec 1 before and after each marker, Slip the last st.

Row 6 . . .   Red—DP across to last st., dec 1 before and after each marker, Slip the last st.

Row 7 . . .   Red—Repeat Row 5.

Row 8 . . .   Red—Repeat Row 6.

Rows 9—14 . . . White—Dec 1 st before and after each marker as you DBK across to the last st., Sl 1.

Rows 15—18 . . . Red—Repeat Rows 5 & 6.

Repeat Rows 1—18 three times more—making a total of 4 pattern repeats.

YOKE: Black

Knit 10 rows in DBK decreasing 2 sts before and after each marker and always slipping the last stitch of each row.

COLLAR: Black

Remove markers as you come to them, knit 25 rows even using the following stitch pattern.

Knit thru the back of three stitches, drop off one and slip one to the right needle. Continue across the row to the last two stitches., BK 1, Sl 1. Should you have three stitches at the end of the first row, dec 1. This is a multiple of 3 plus 2 pattern.

Bind-off by passing 1 st over 3 sts.

FINISHING: Work in yarn ends. Hand sew the 24″ zipper up the front of the poncho. The collar is so tightly knit that it curls automatically. No amount of blocking will make it remain uncurled. Should you desire a collar that will not curl, TBK each row instead of using the pattern listed above. Block.

THE GAUCHO PONCHO

MATERIAL: 10—50 gram Balls Spinnerin Toros
1 pr. #17 (½″) Needles
½ yd. matching color suede

GAUGE: 3 sts = 1″   2 rows = 1″

BACK:

Double Knit-On 60 sts.

Row 1 . . . DBK across to last st., Sl 1.

Row 2 . . . DP across to last st., Sl 1.

Repeat Rows 1 & 2 until piece measures 30″ (or desired length).

There are now 90 rows worked.

Row 91 . . . DBK 21, Bind-off 18 in DBK, DBK 20, Sl 1.

Row 92 . . . DP across to last three sts, inc 1, DP 1, Sl 1.

Attach separate ball of yarn at opposite neck edge . . . Inc 1 in 1st st, DP across to last two sts, DP 1, Sl 1.

Row 93 . . . DBK across to last three sts, inc 1 in next st., DBK 1, Sl 1. Left Front . . . Inc 1 in 1st DBK st, DBK across to last st., Sl 1.

Rows 94—100 . . . Repeat Rows 92 and 93 ending with a repeat of Row 92. There are now 30 sts on the left and the right fronts.

Work even for 20″ repeating Rows 1 & 2. Bind-off in pattern.

FINISHING: Cut one piece of suede 20″ x 7″ and two pieces of suede 10″ x 7″. Cut ¼″ strips of fringe leaving ½″ across the top of each piece for attaching to poncho. Also cut 1″ strips of suede for binding the outside edges and the edges up the front and around the neck. Work in yarn ends. The poncho is reversible if the yarn ends are properly worked into the knit. When wearing, the back should hang approximately 6″ longer than the front.

SKINNY BELTS

Fig. 1—Belt is made of Reynold's Patte de Velours—#15 Needles. Cast-on 260 sts using any method of cast-on desired. Slip two sts to the right needle and pass 1 st over the other st. Continue slipping one stitch at a time and passing 1 stitch over the other stitch. Secure yarn ends. Cut 24 strands of 24″ each. Using 12 strands per tassel, attach one to each end of the belt.

Fig. 2—Belt is made of Bernat's OpalSpun—Red, White and Blue Colors—½″ Needles. Using the instructions as in Fig. 1, casting-on as many stitches as the needle will hold, make three belts—one in each color. Stretch the belts & block them. Secure the three ends together and braid them. Make large tassels using the three colors and secure to each end of the belt.

Fig. 3—Belt is made of Spinnerin's Entice—#15 Needles. Double Knit-On 300 sts., Bind-off as you DBK across the knit-on sts. Bind-off by passing 1 st over 1 st. Attach exceptionally long strands to each end of the belt. These are approximately 12″ long and are not cut on the ends.

Fig. 4—BRACELET—Spinnerin's Entice—#11 Needles— Double Knit-On 12 sts. Work in Herringbone Stitch Pattern until strip is long enough to circle a plastic wrist bracelet. Sew ends of the strip together, place around plastic bracelet and slip the edges together on the inside rim of bracelet. Spray with clear laquer to protect from dirt and damage.